QUAINT CATS

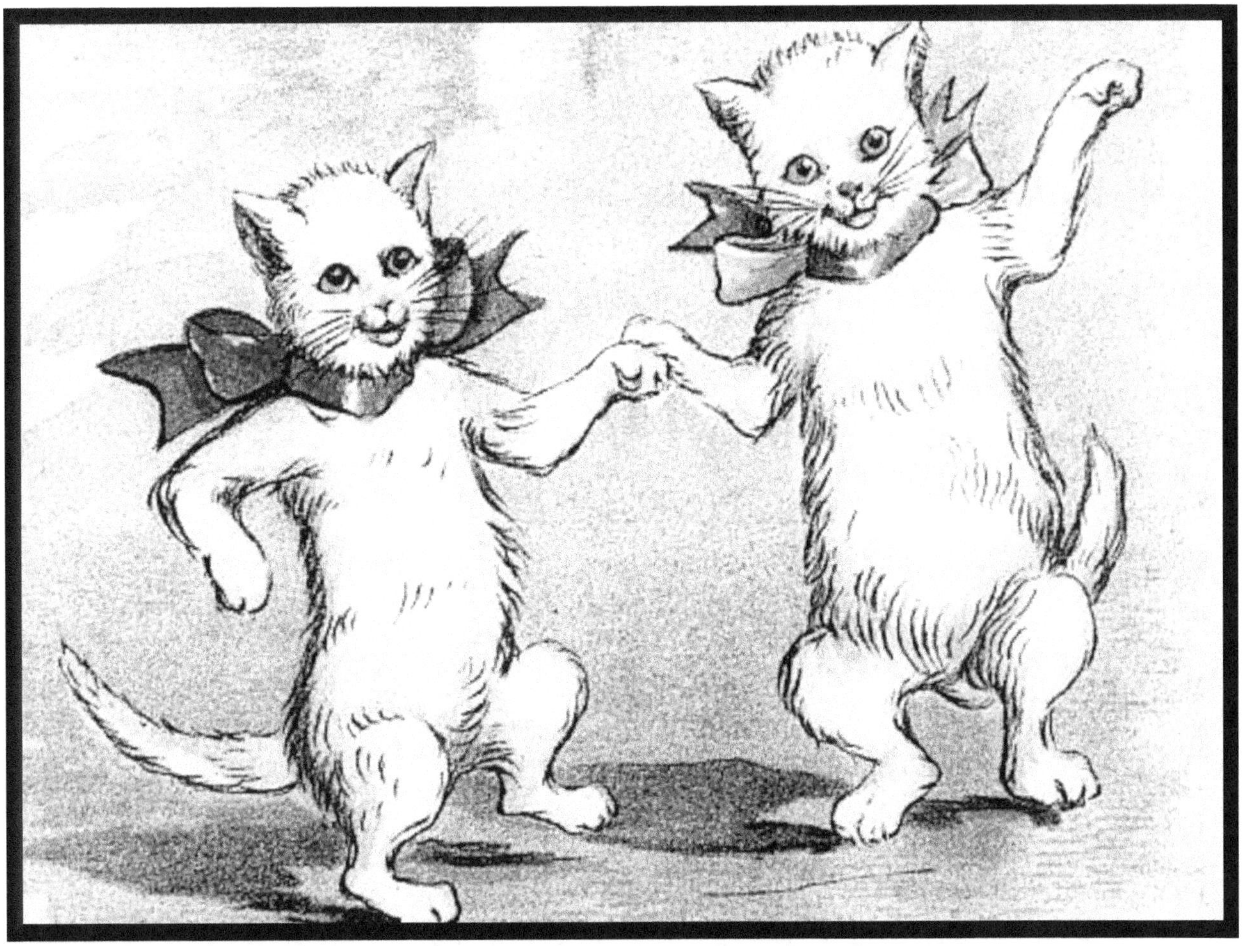

GRAYSCALE ADULT COLORING BOOK

OLDE GLORIE STUDIOS

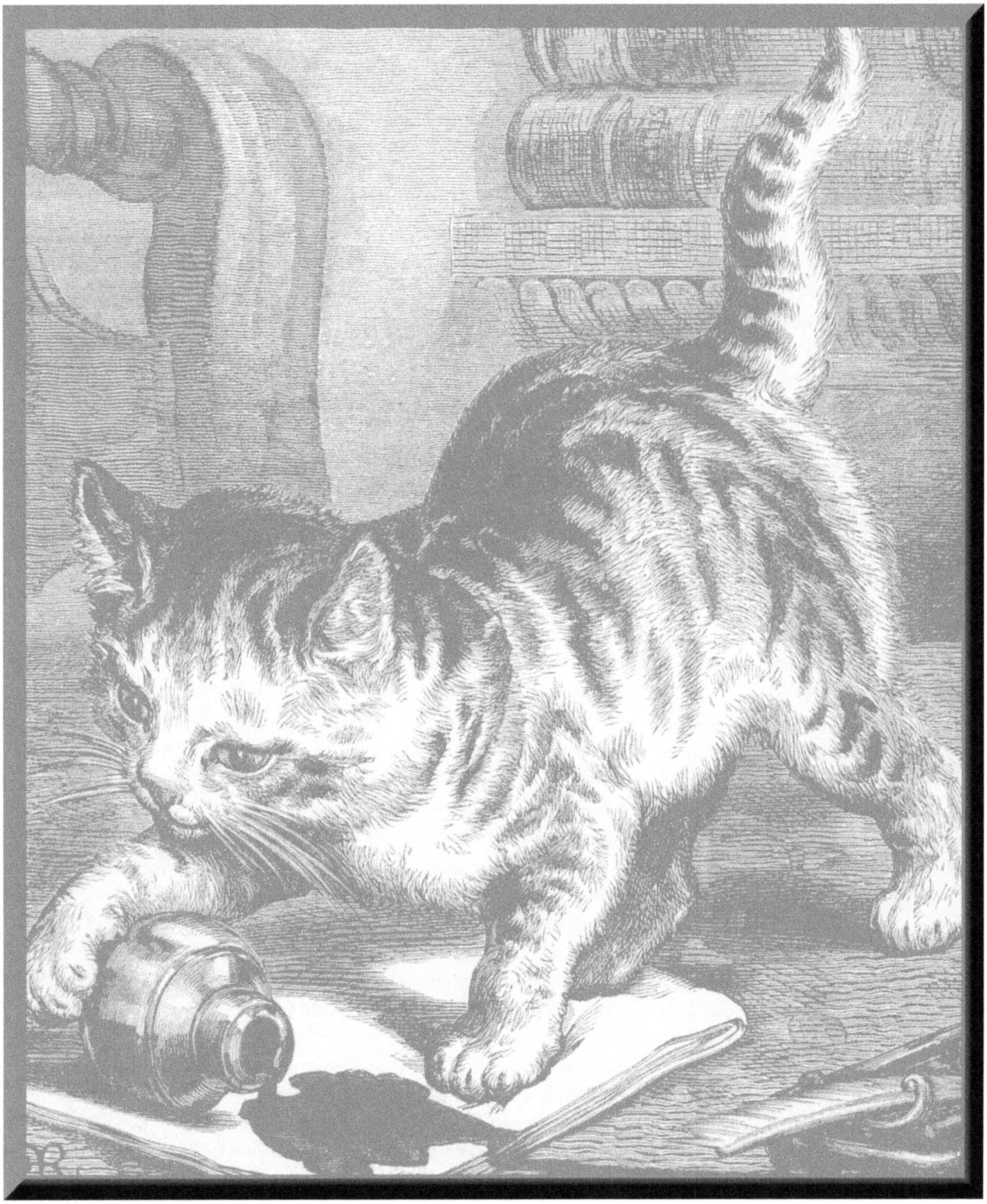

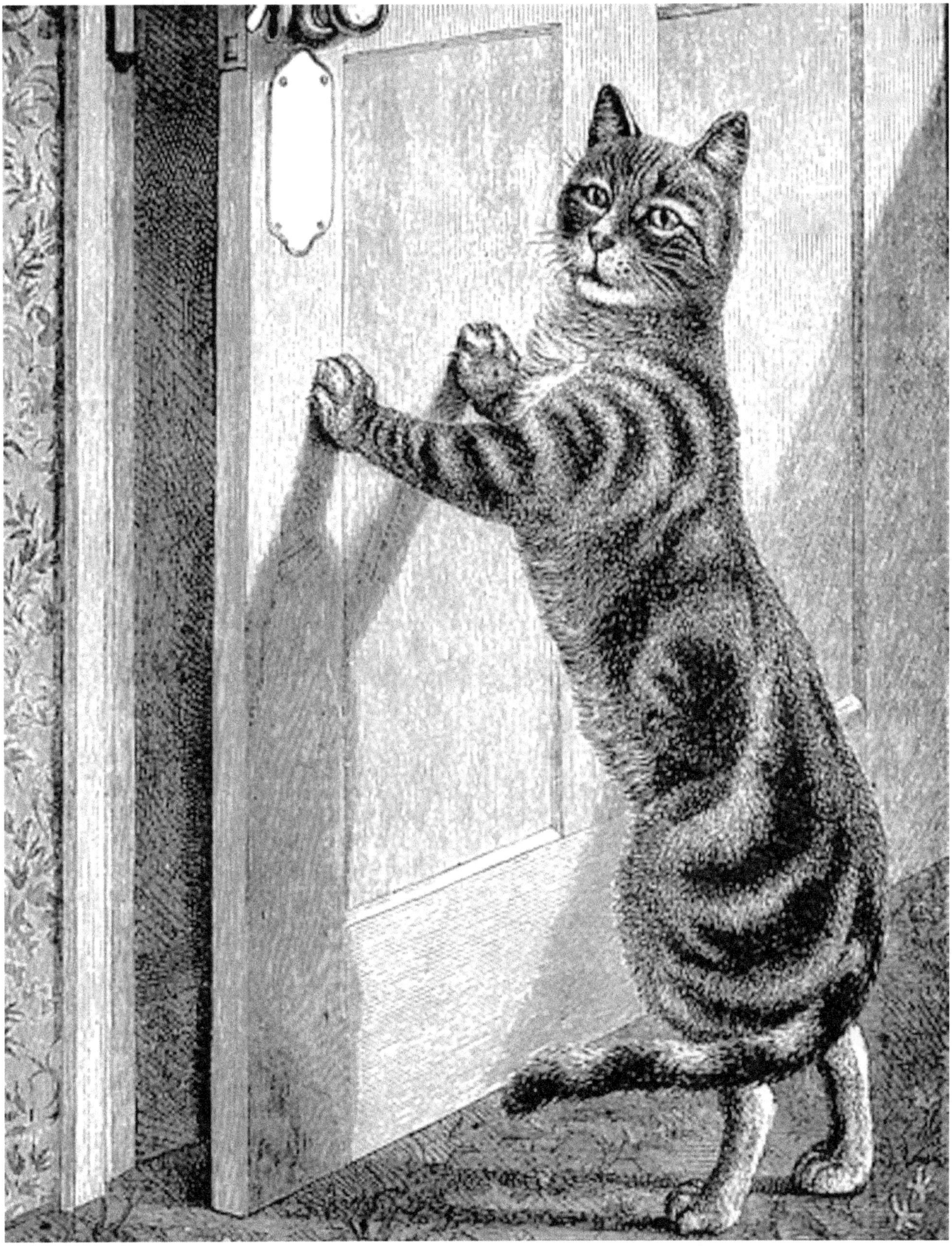

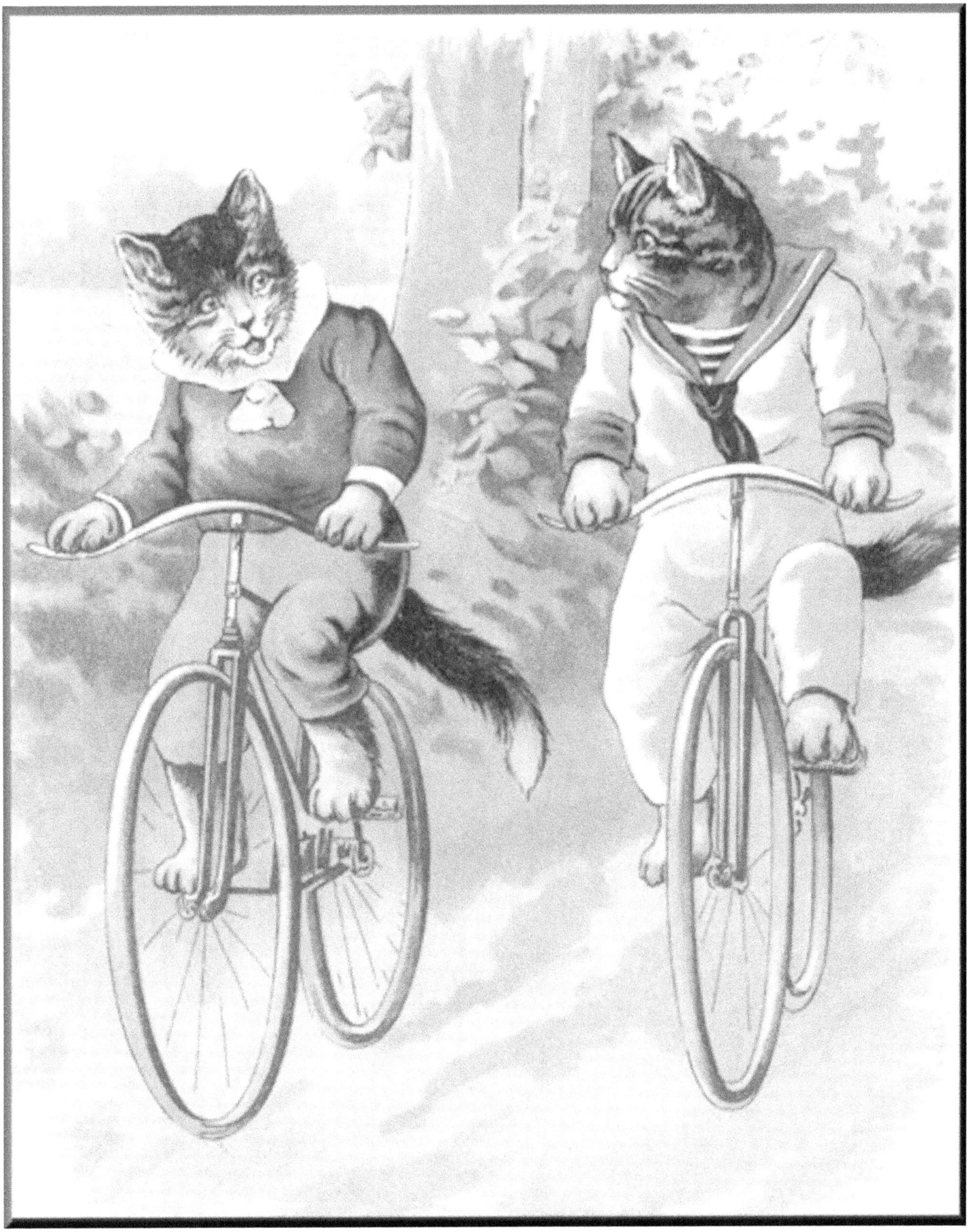

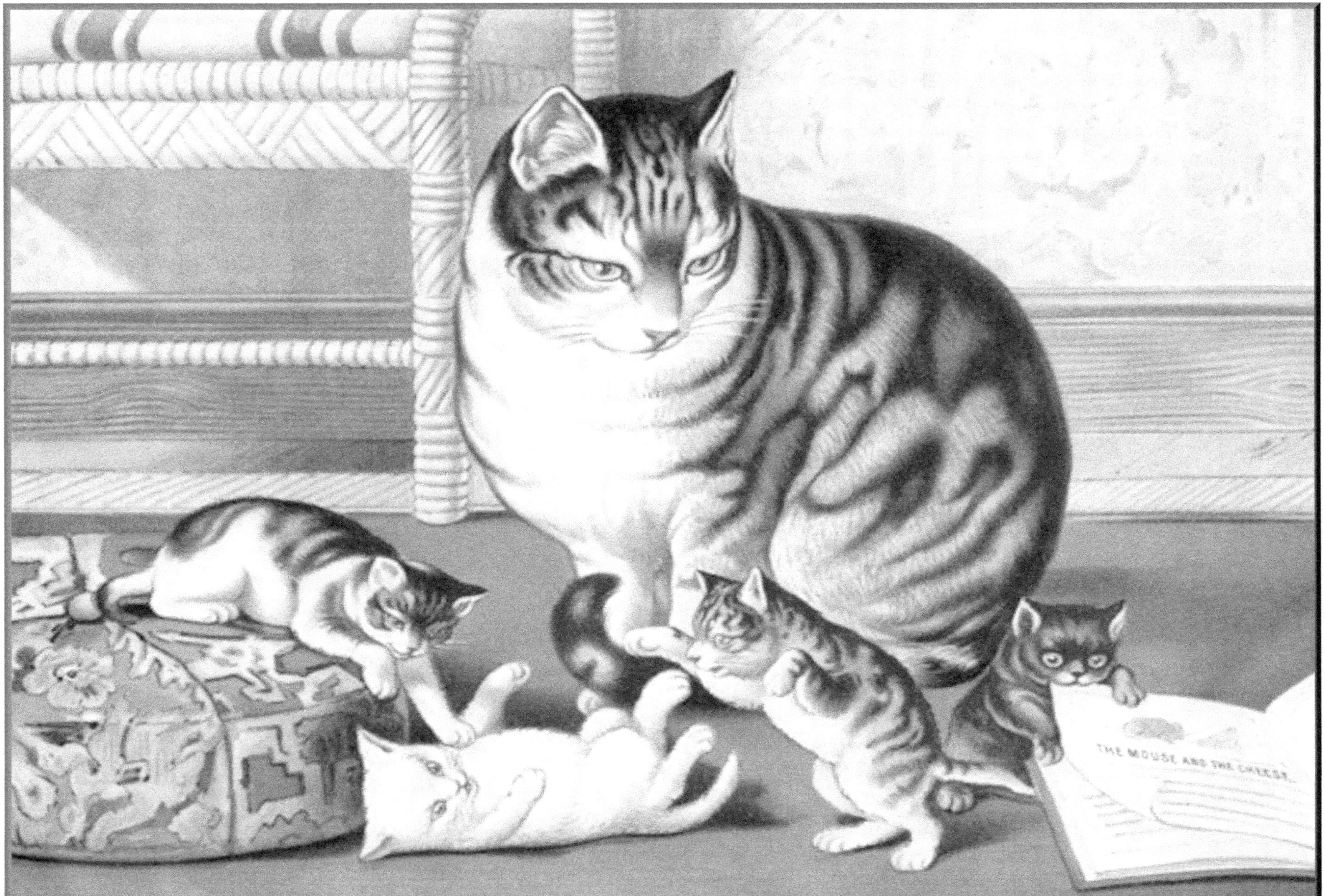
THE MOUSE AND THE CHEESE.

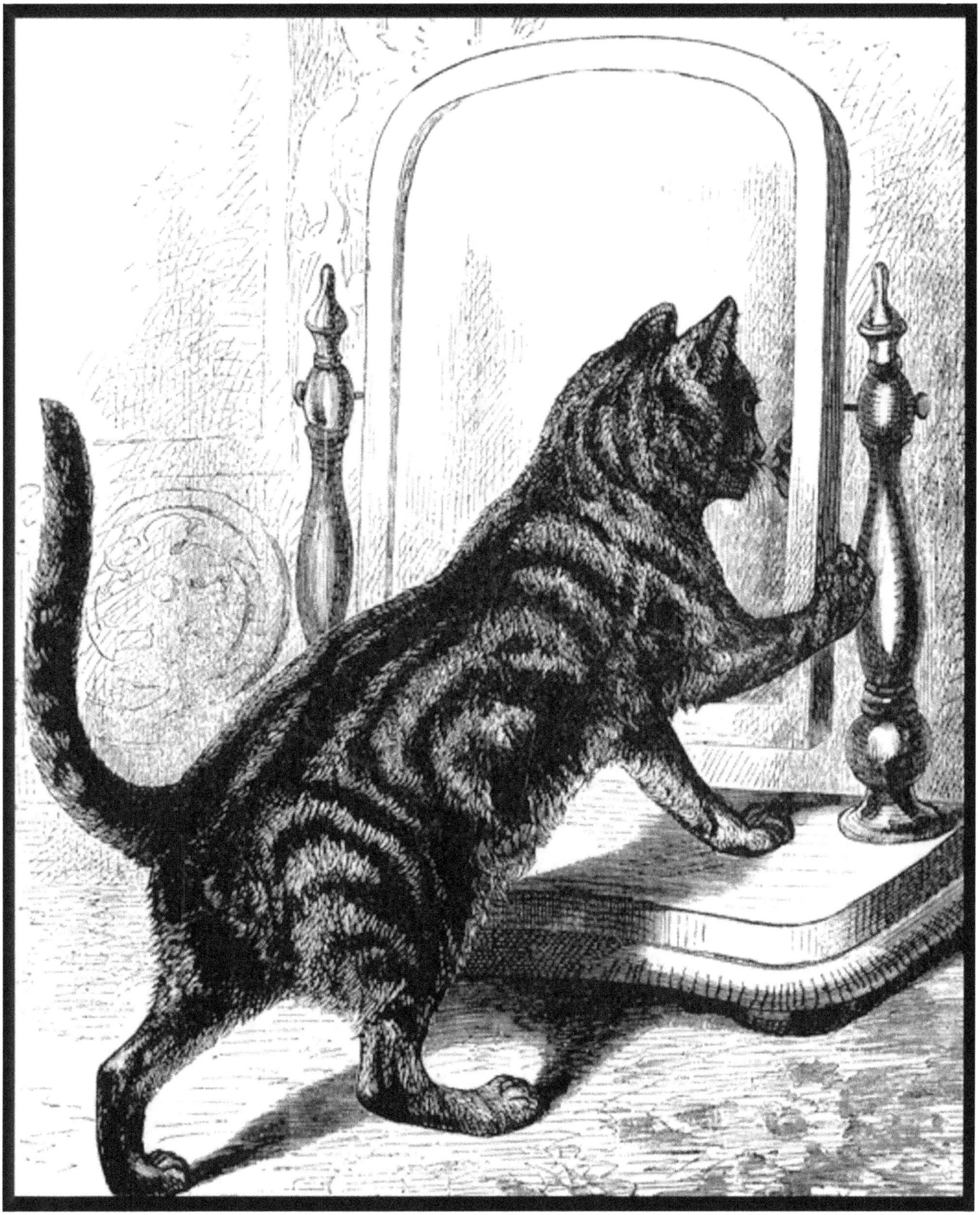

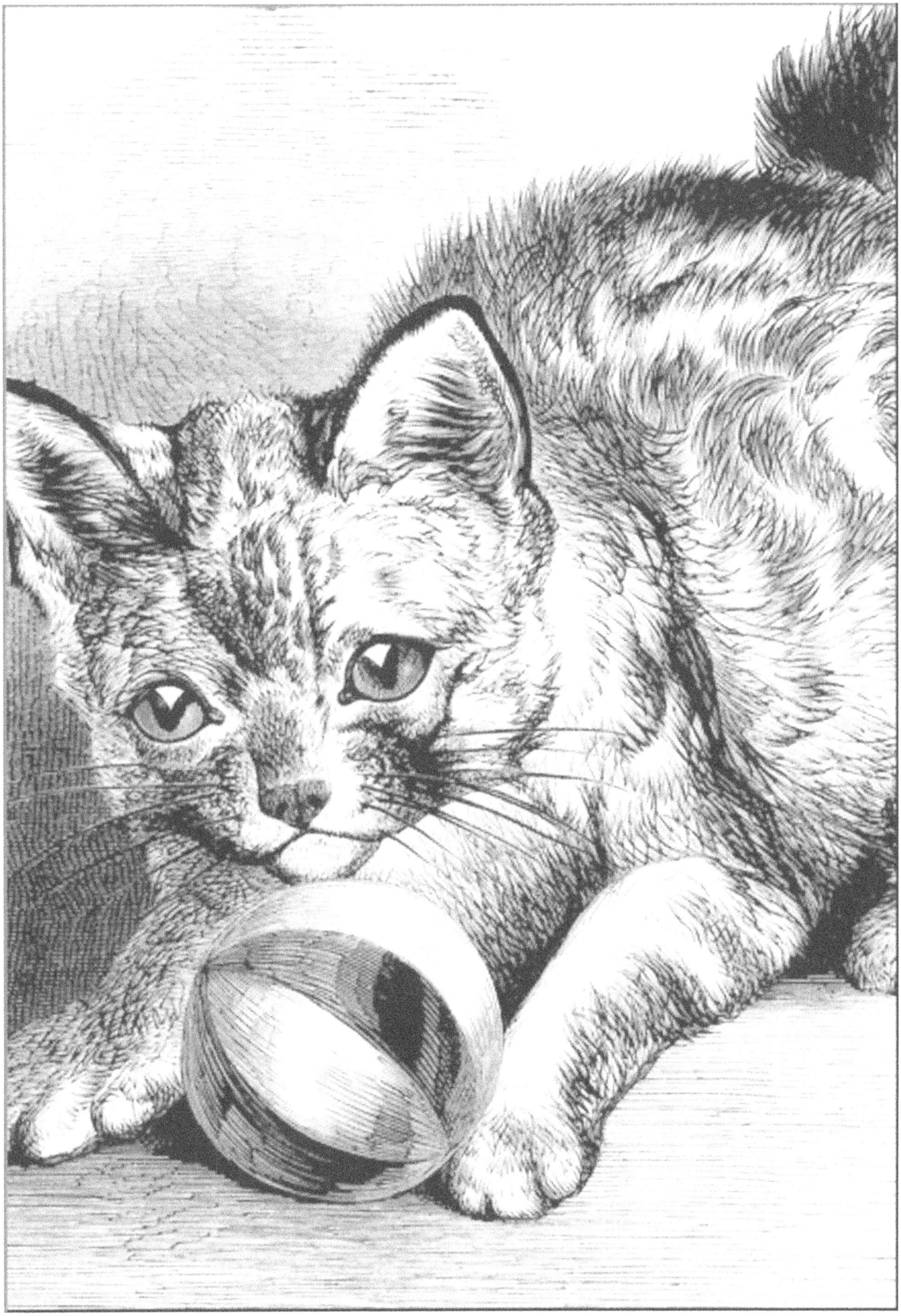

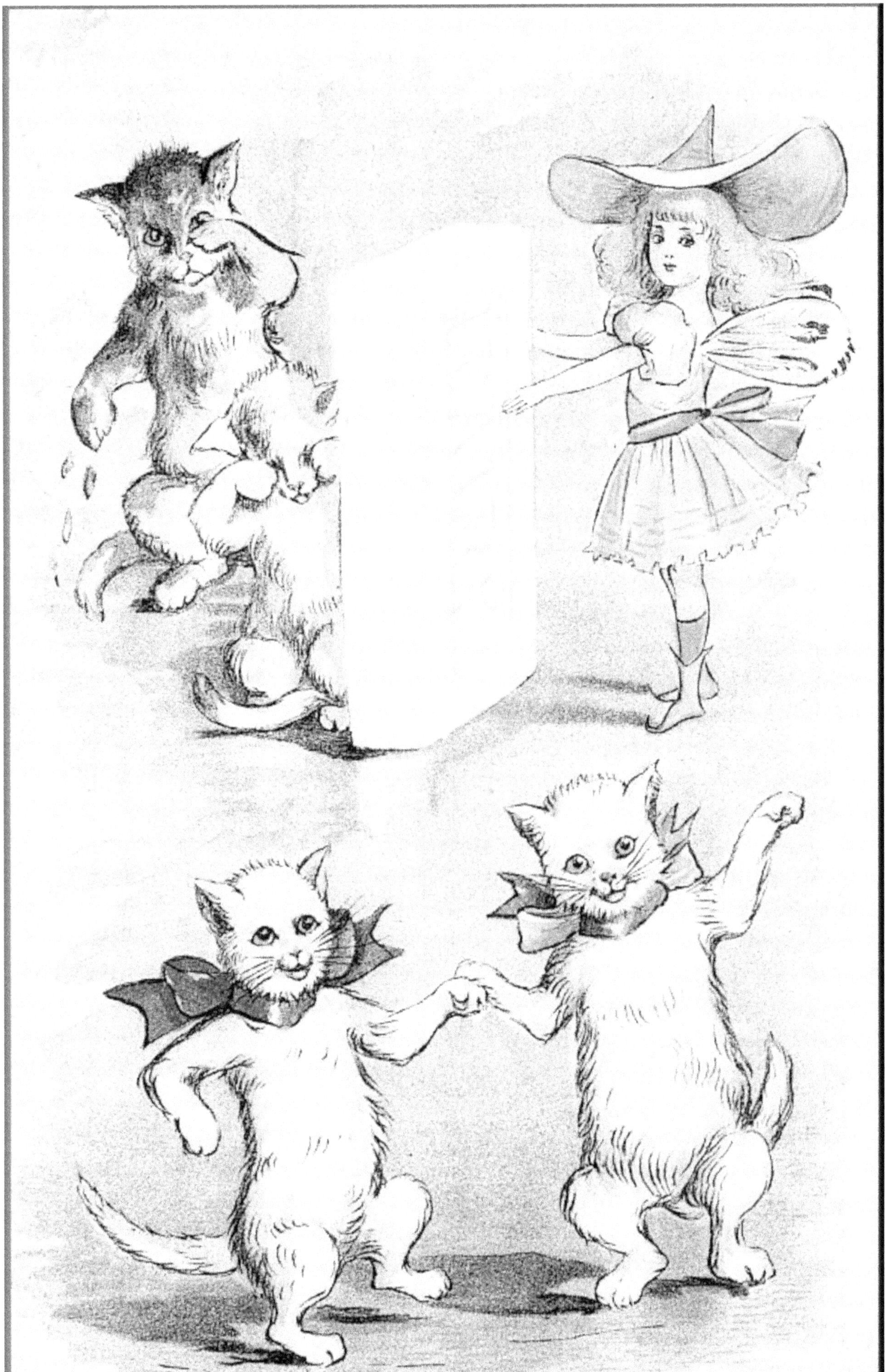

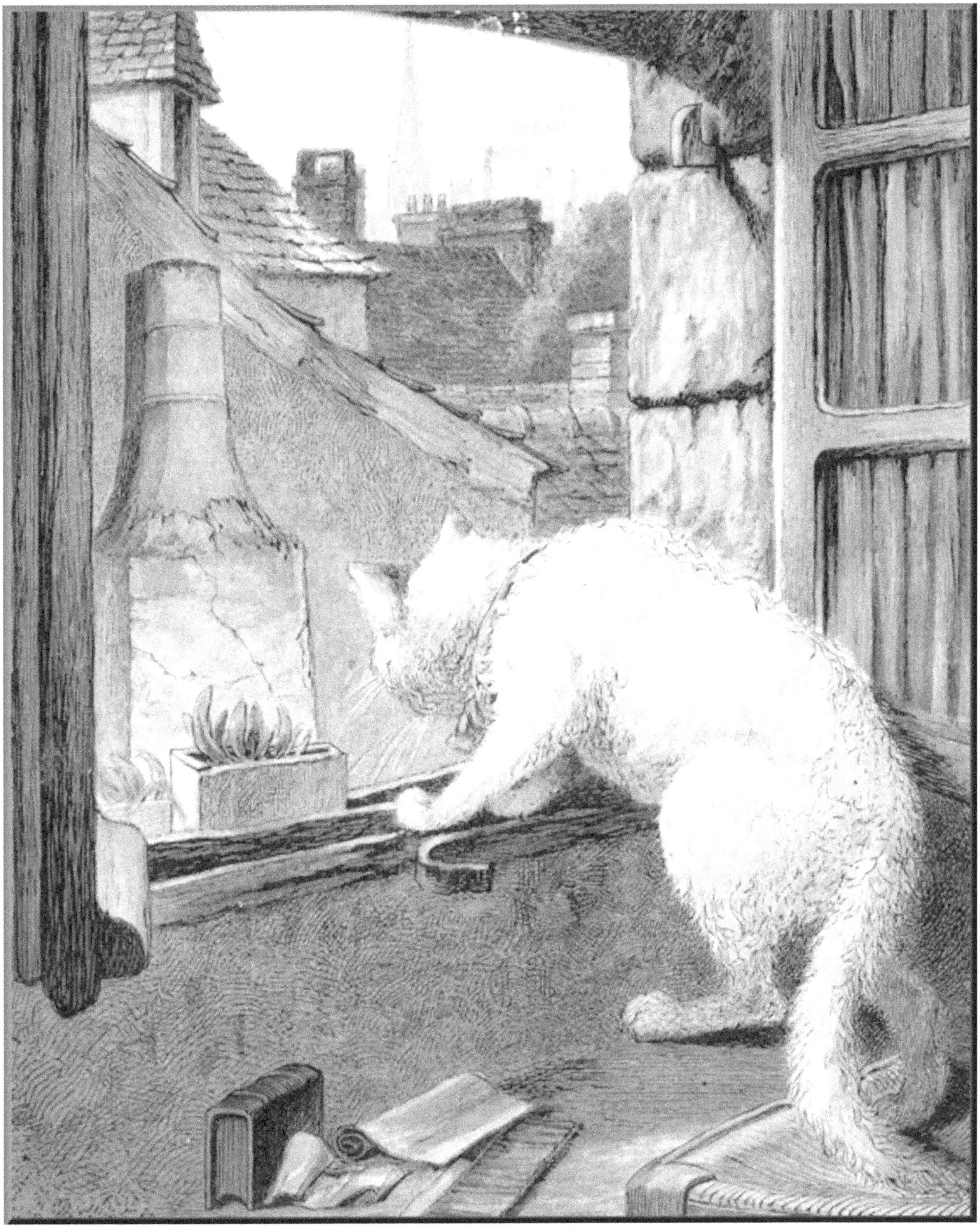

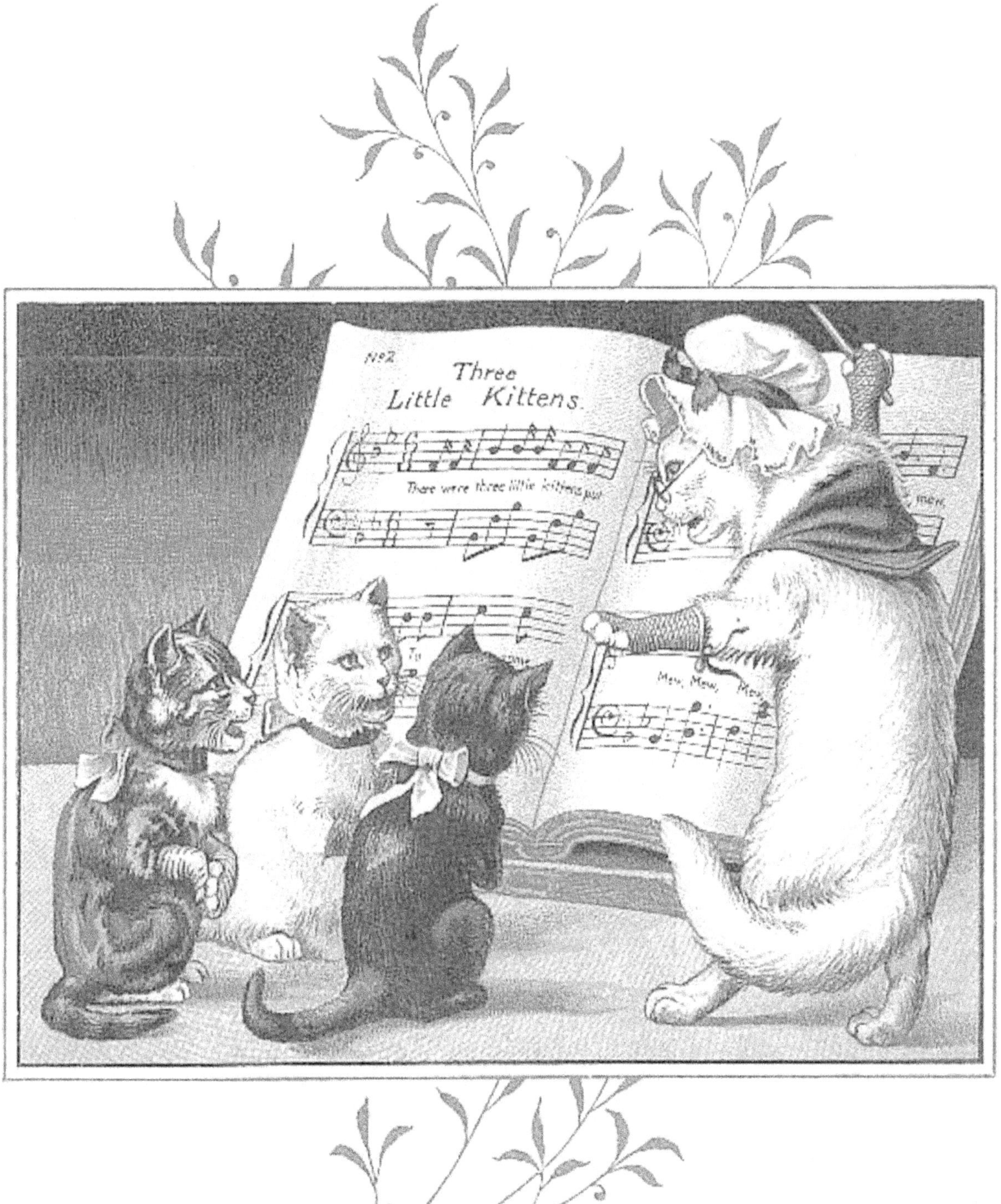

Three
Little Kittens.
There were three little kittens put
Mew, Mew, Mew

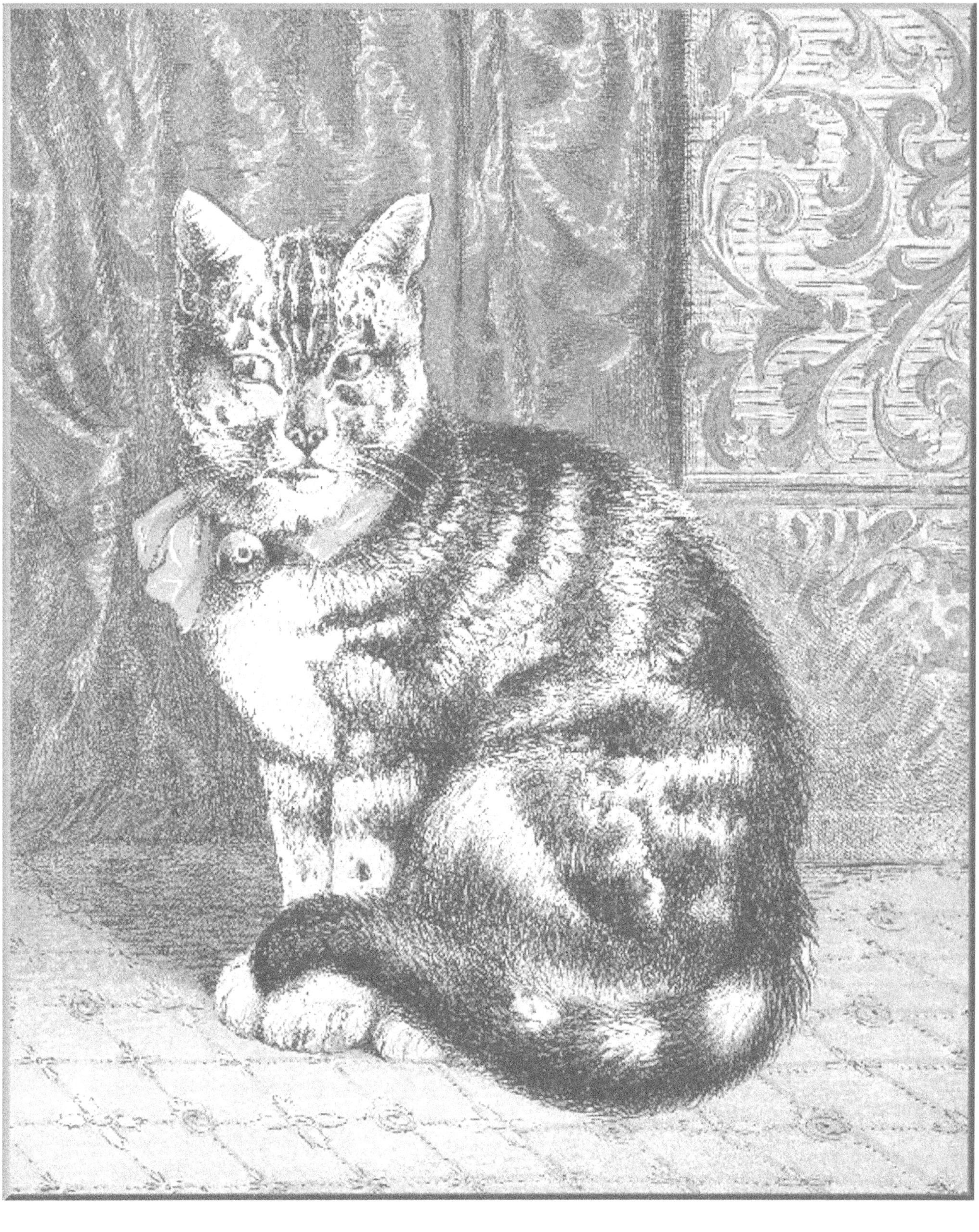

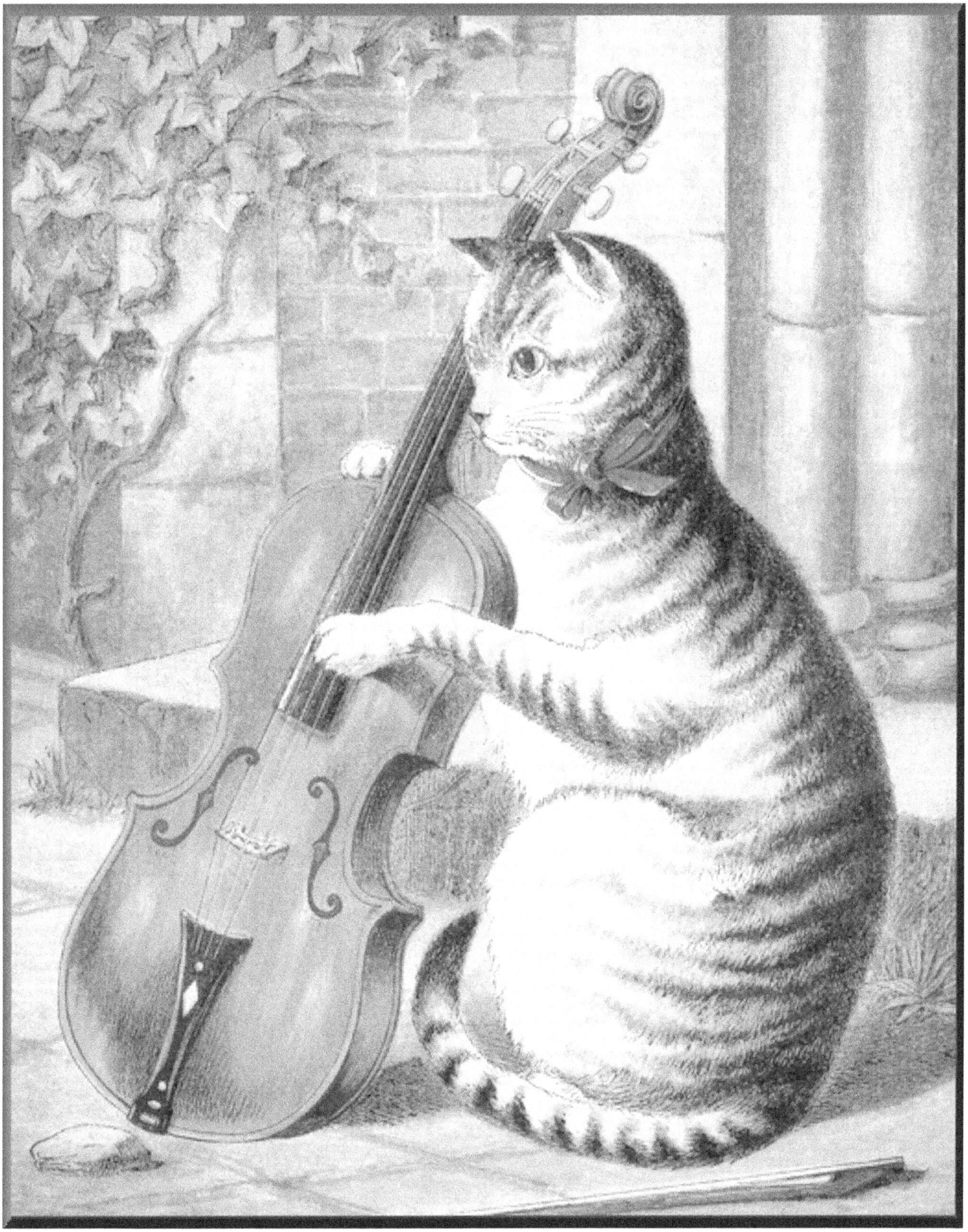

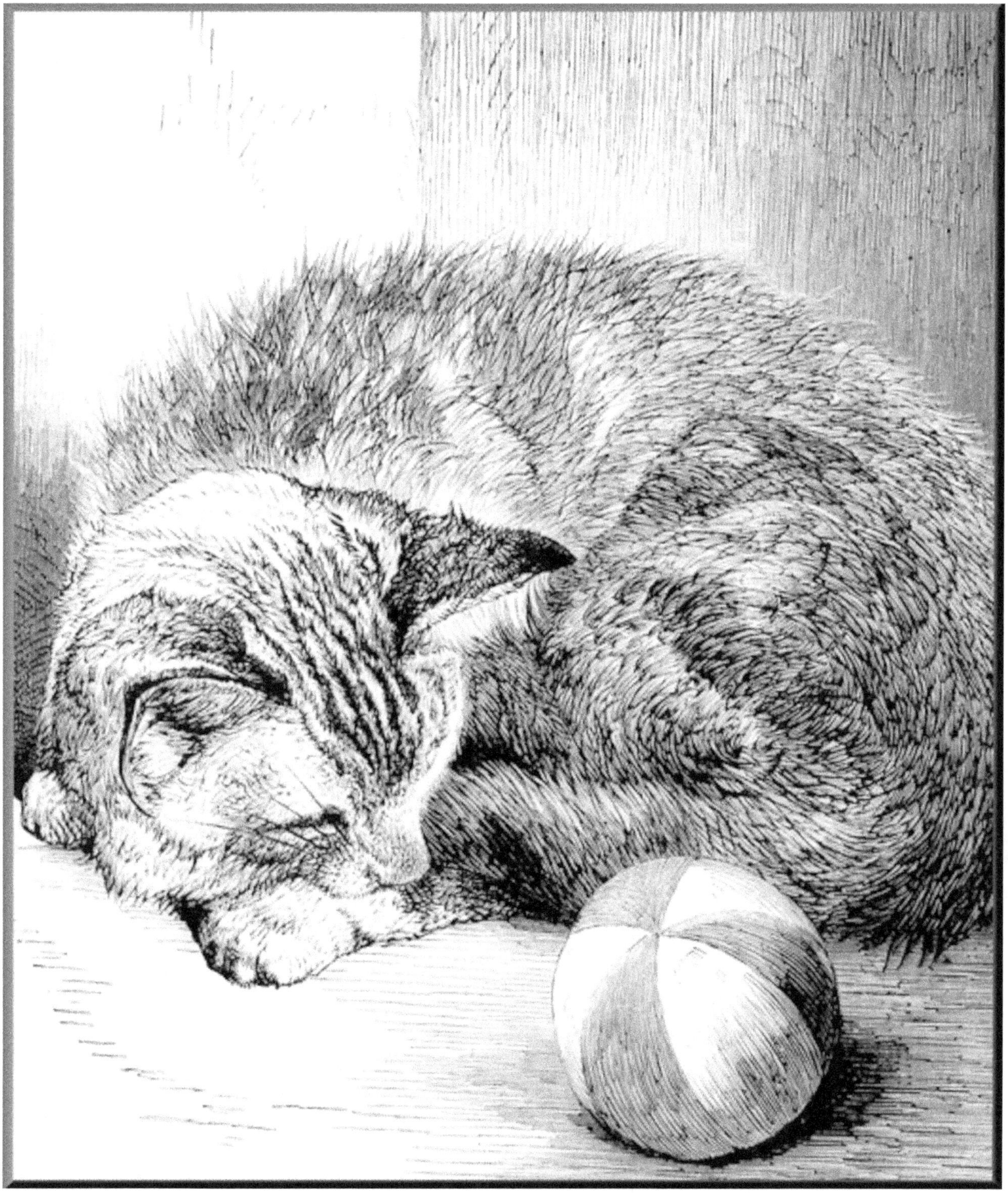

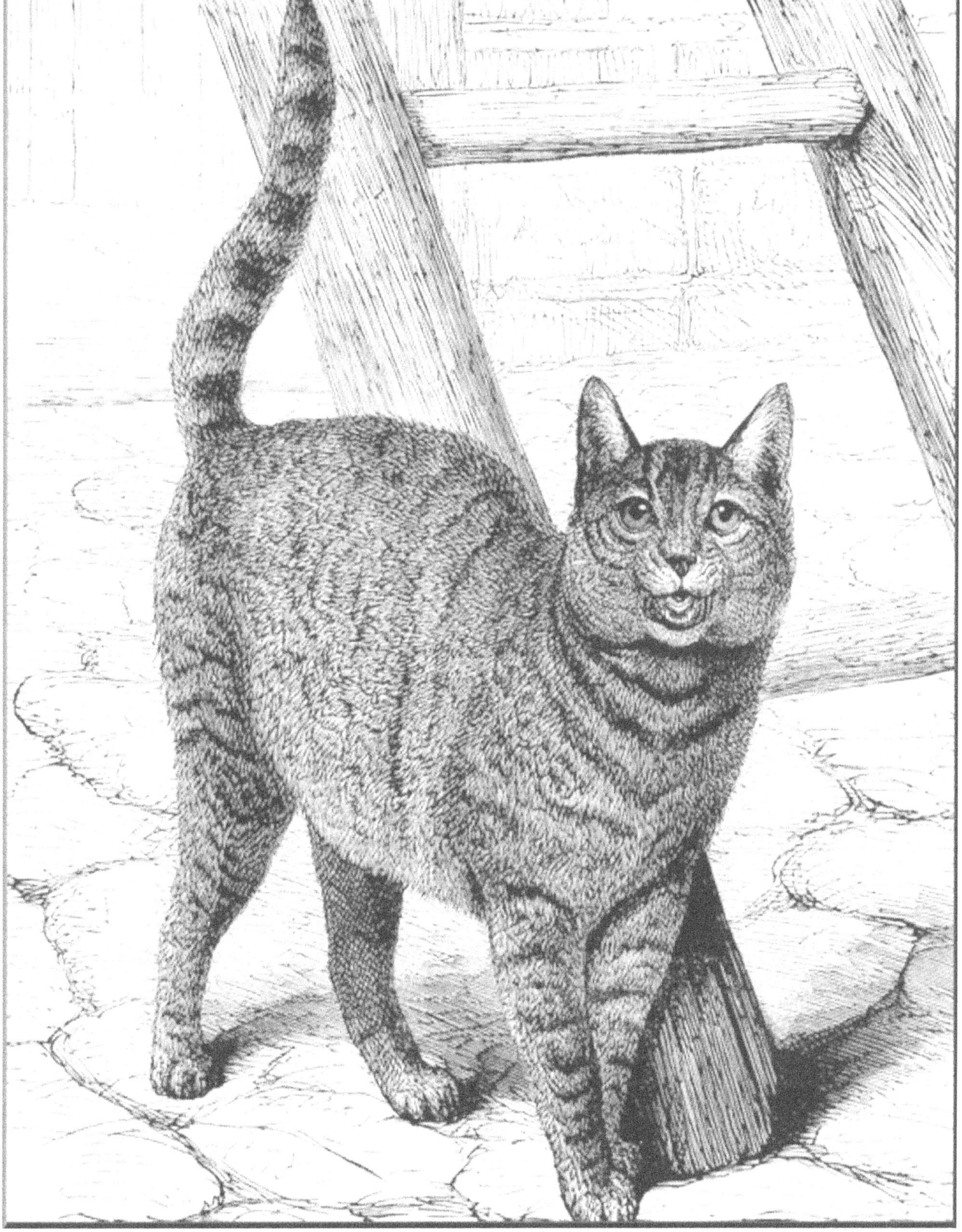

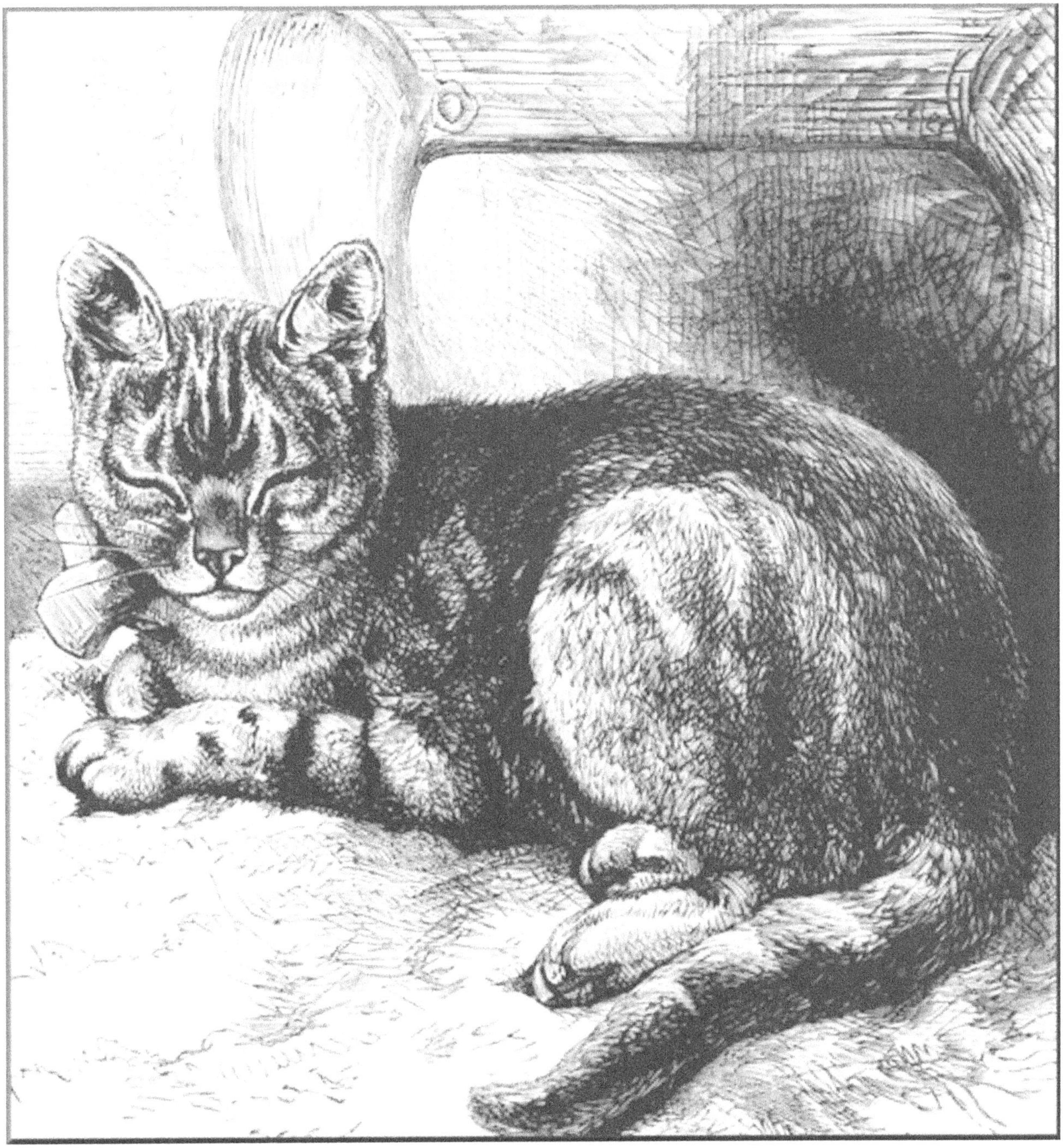

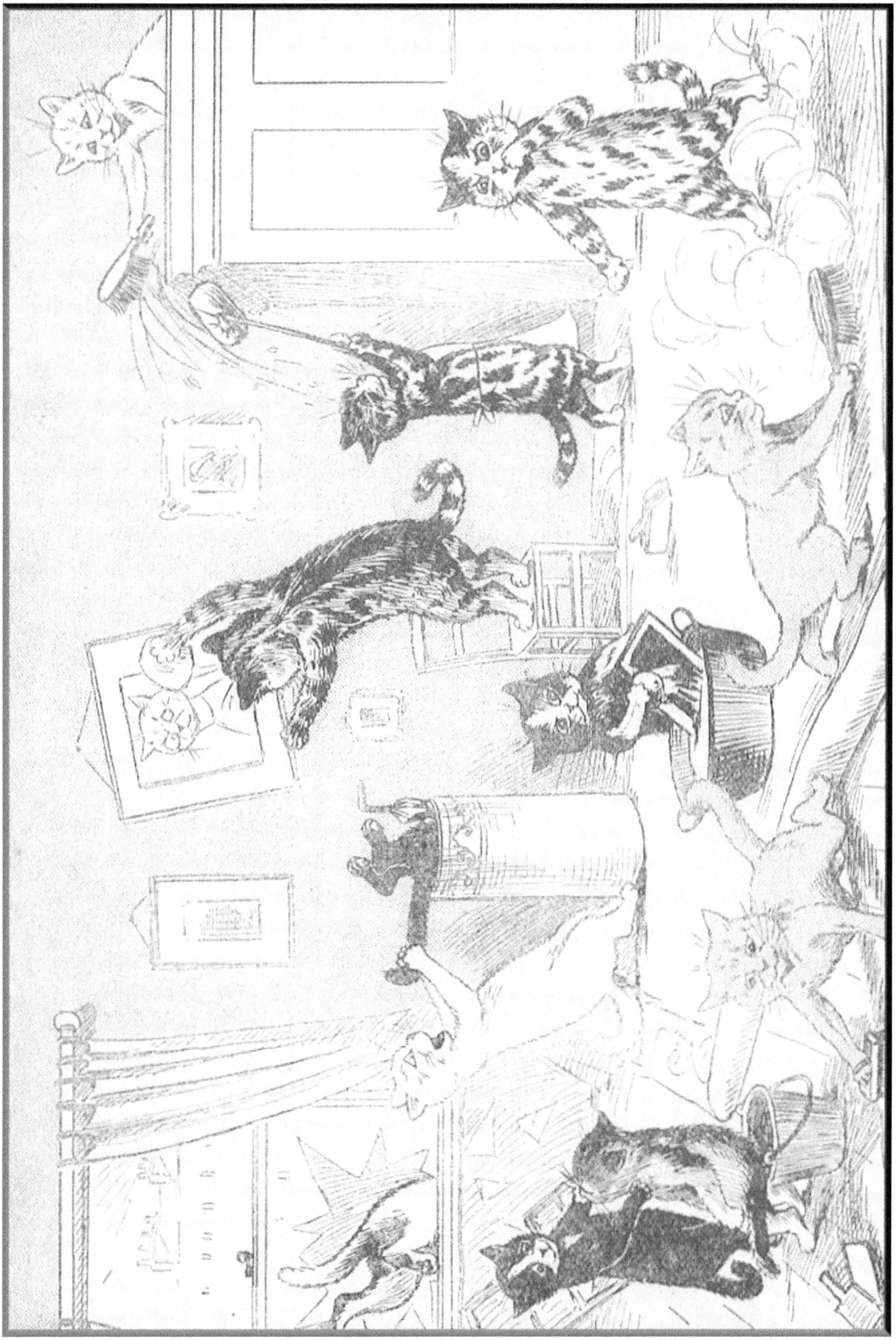

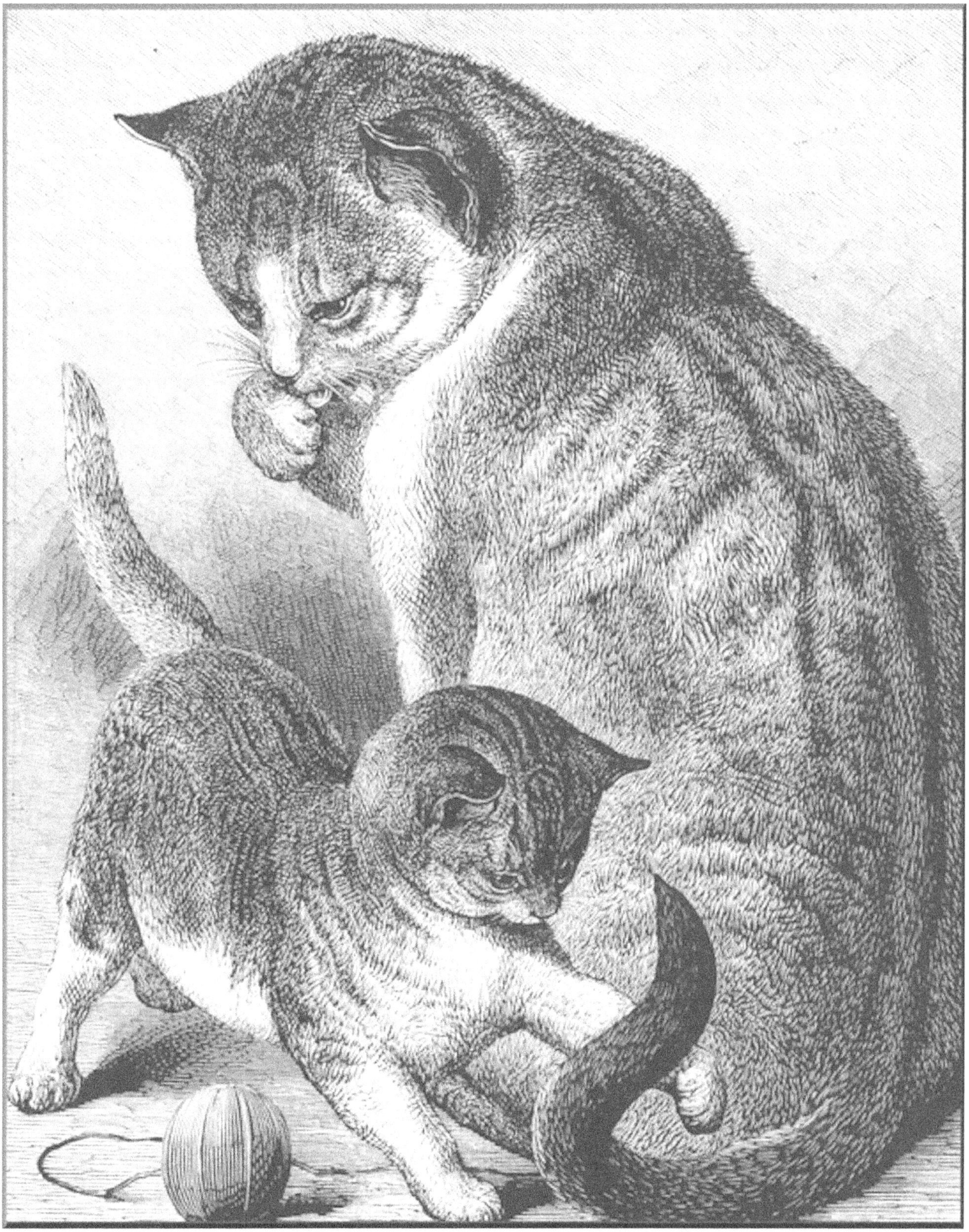

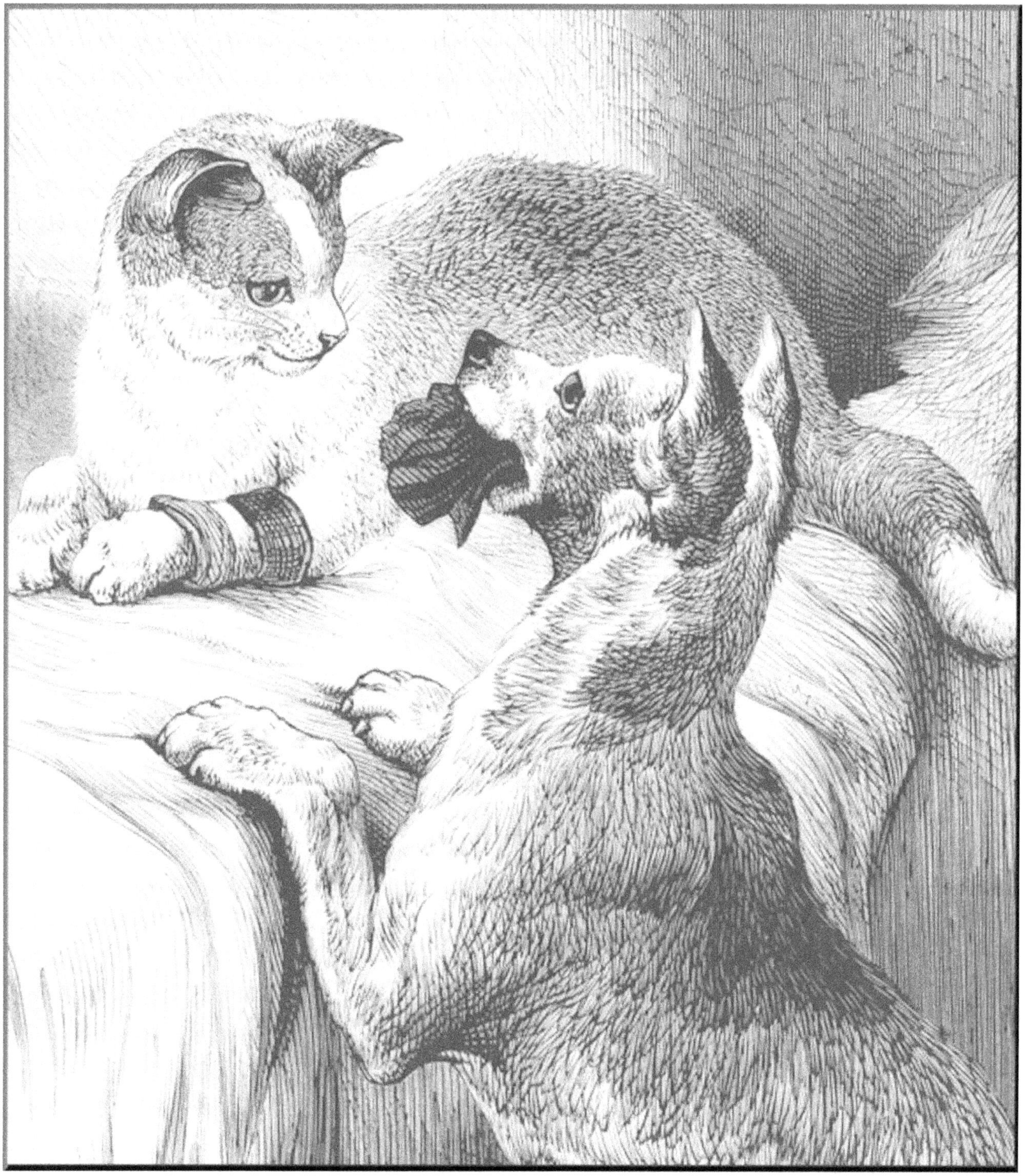

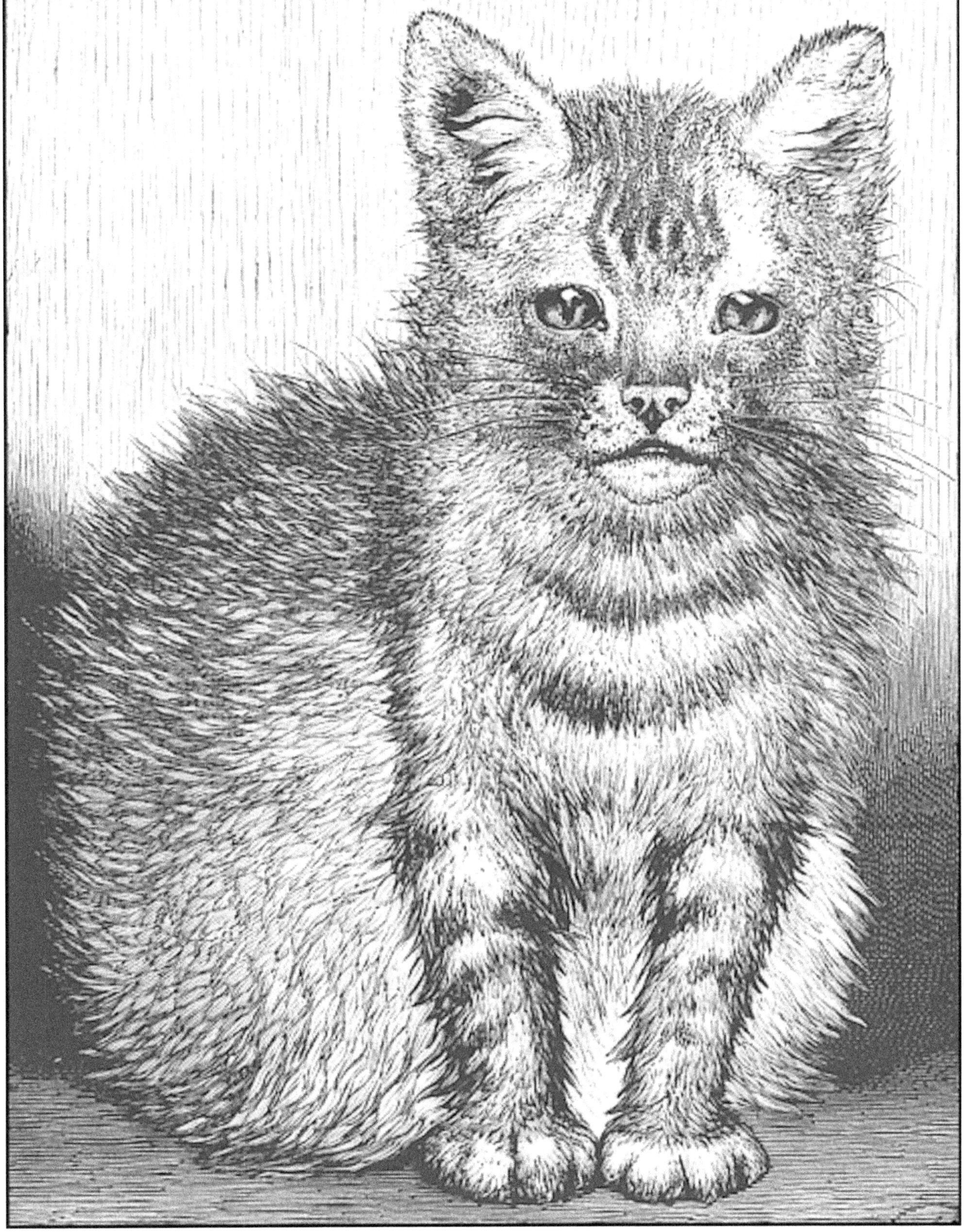

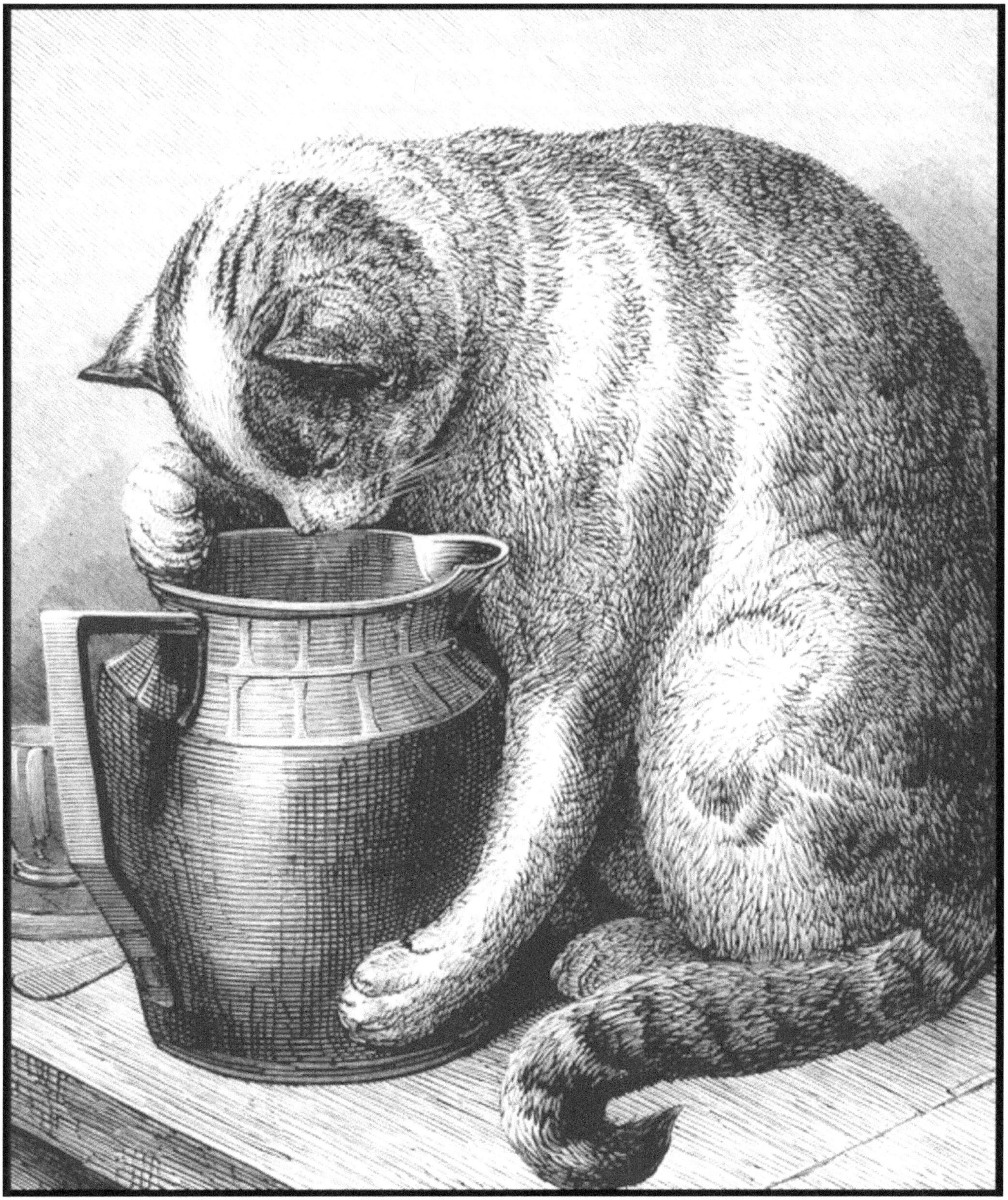

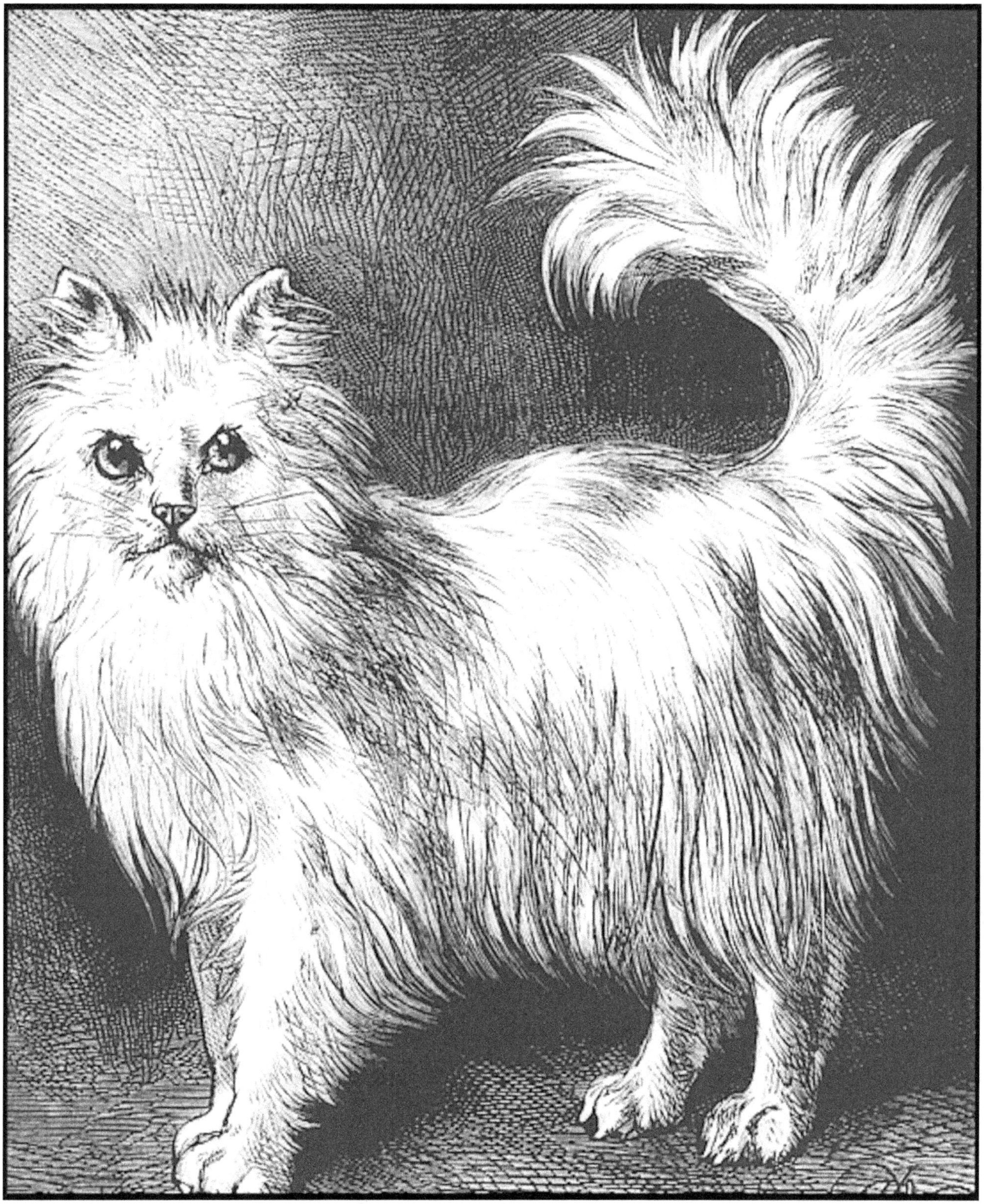

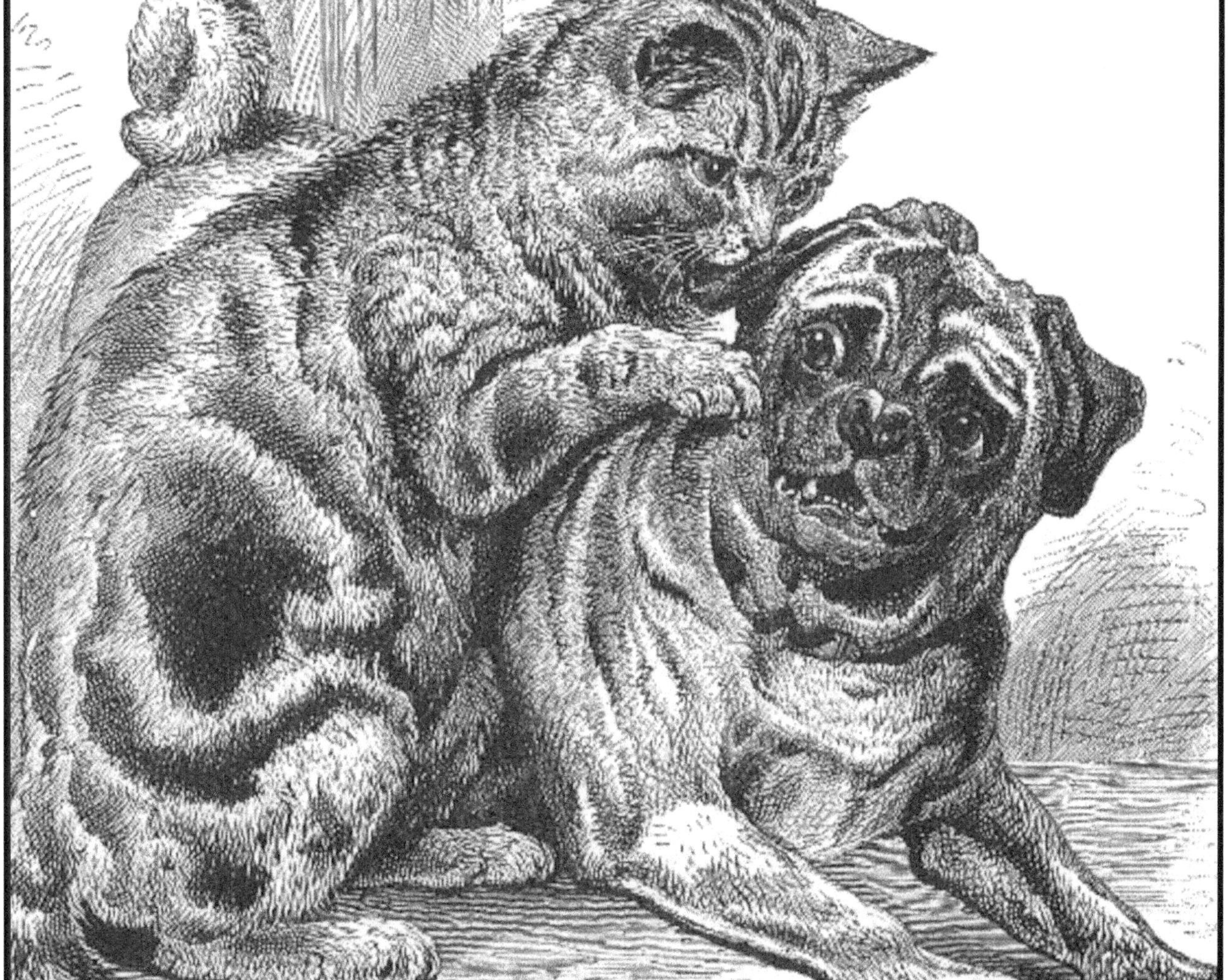

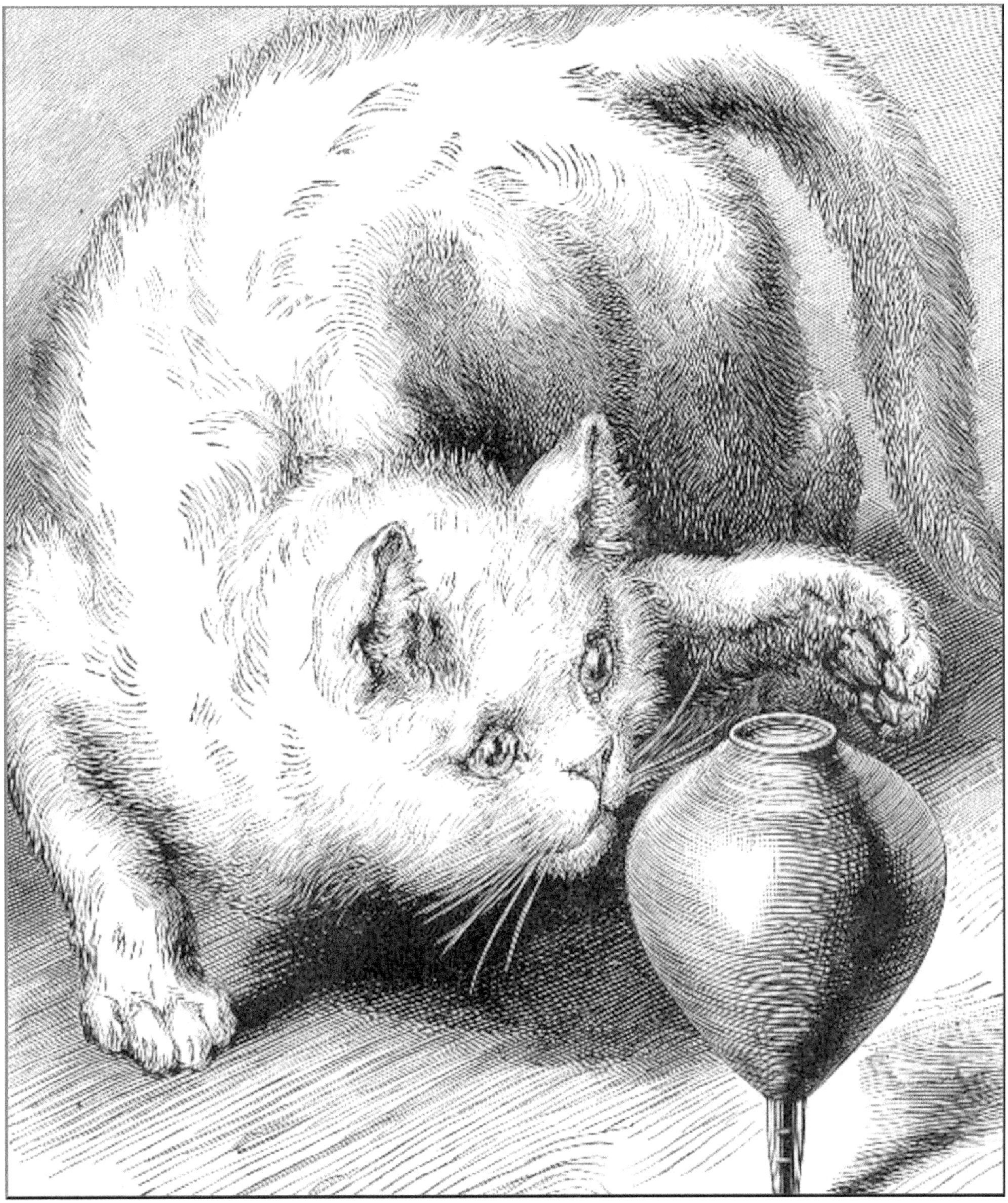

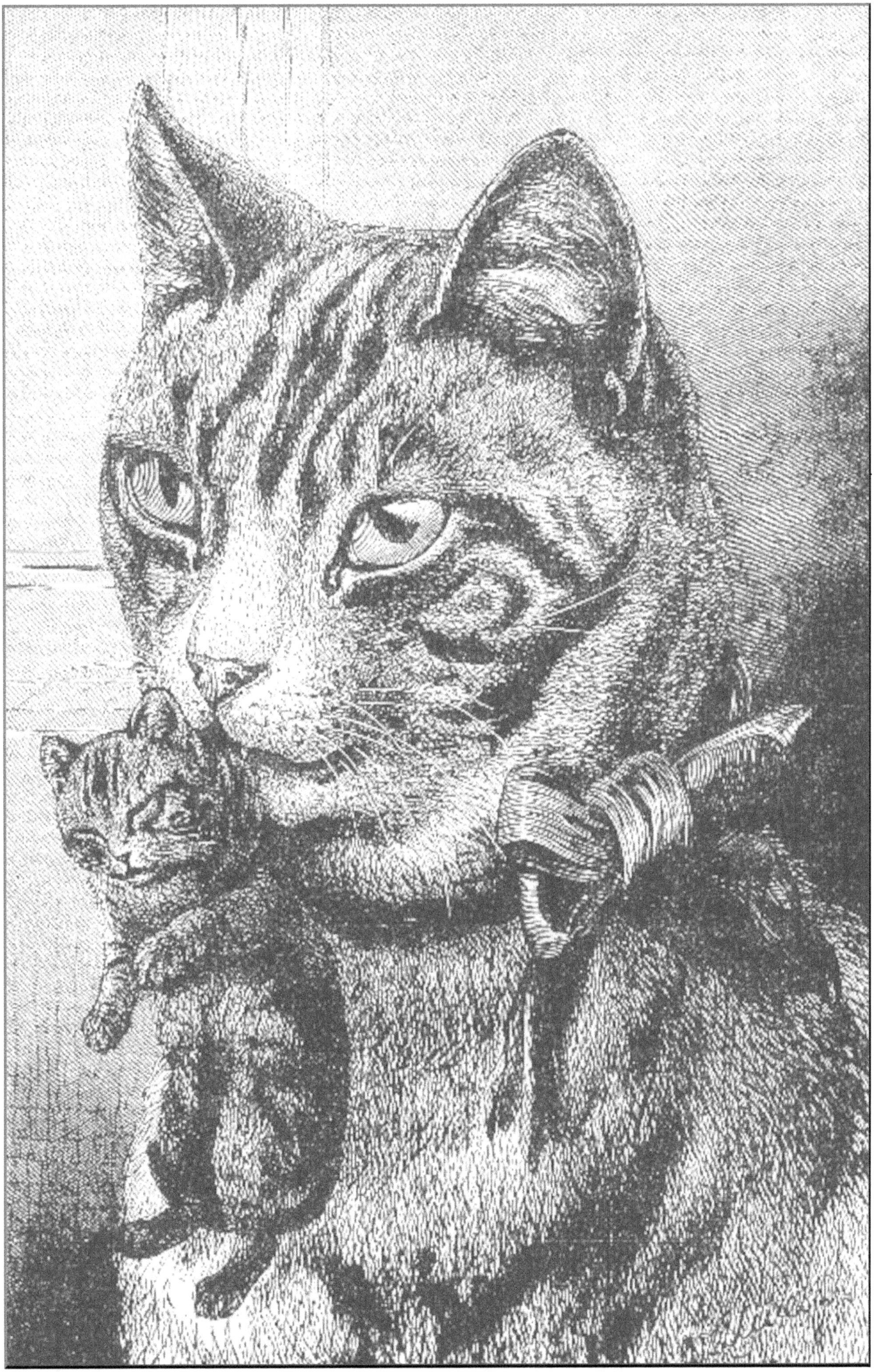

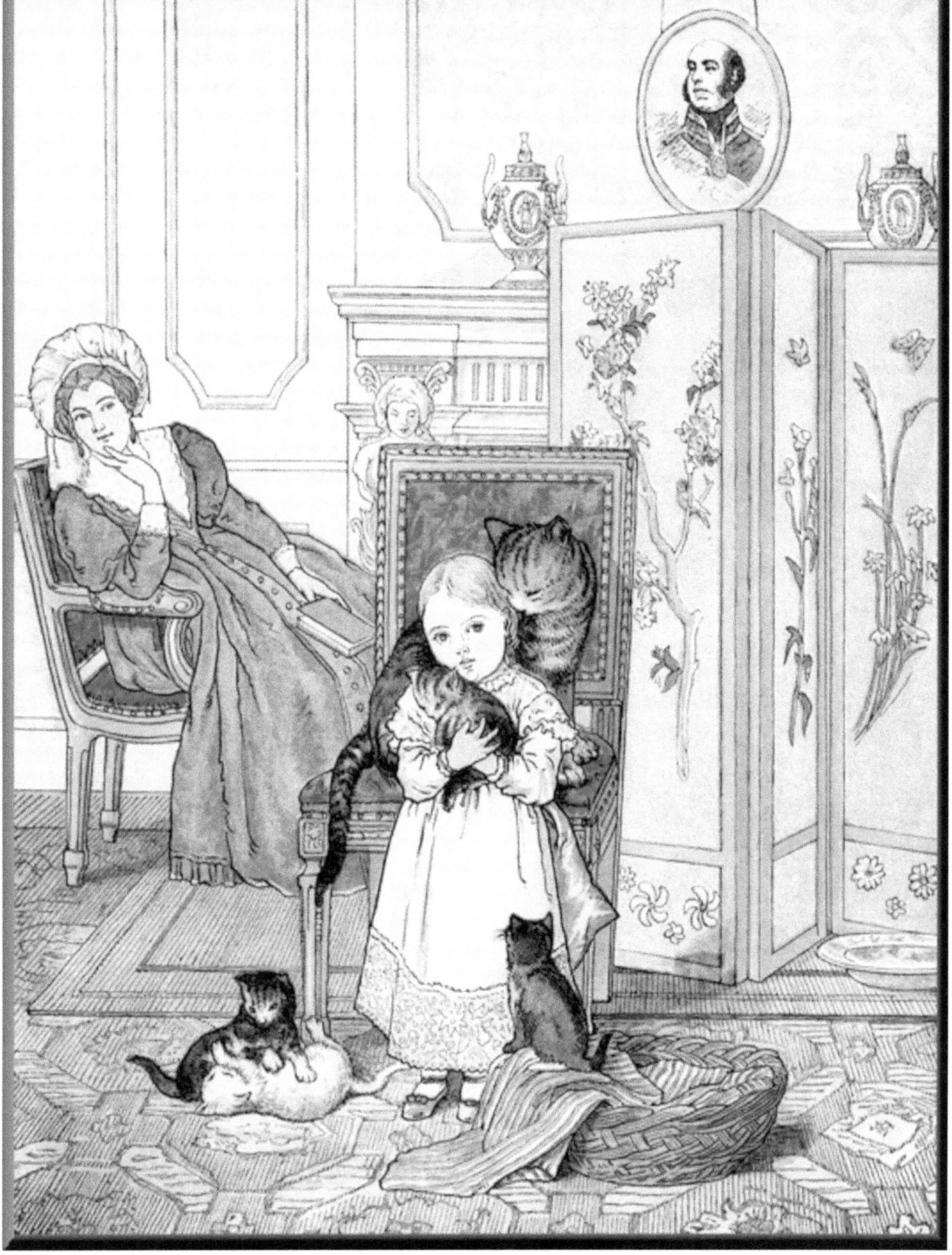

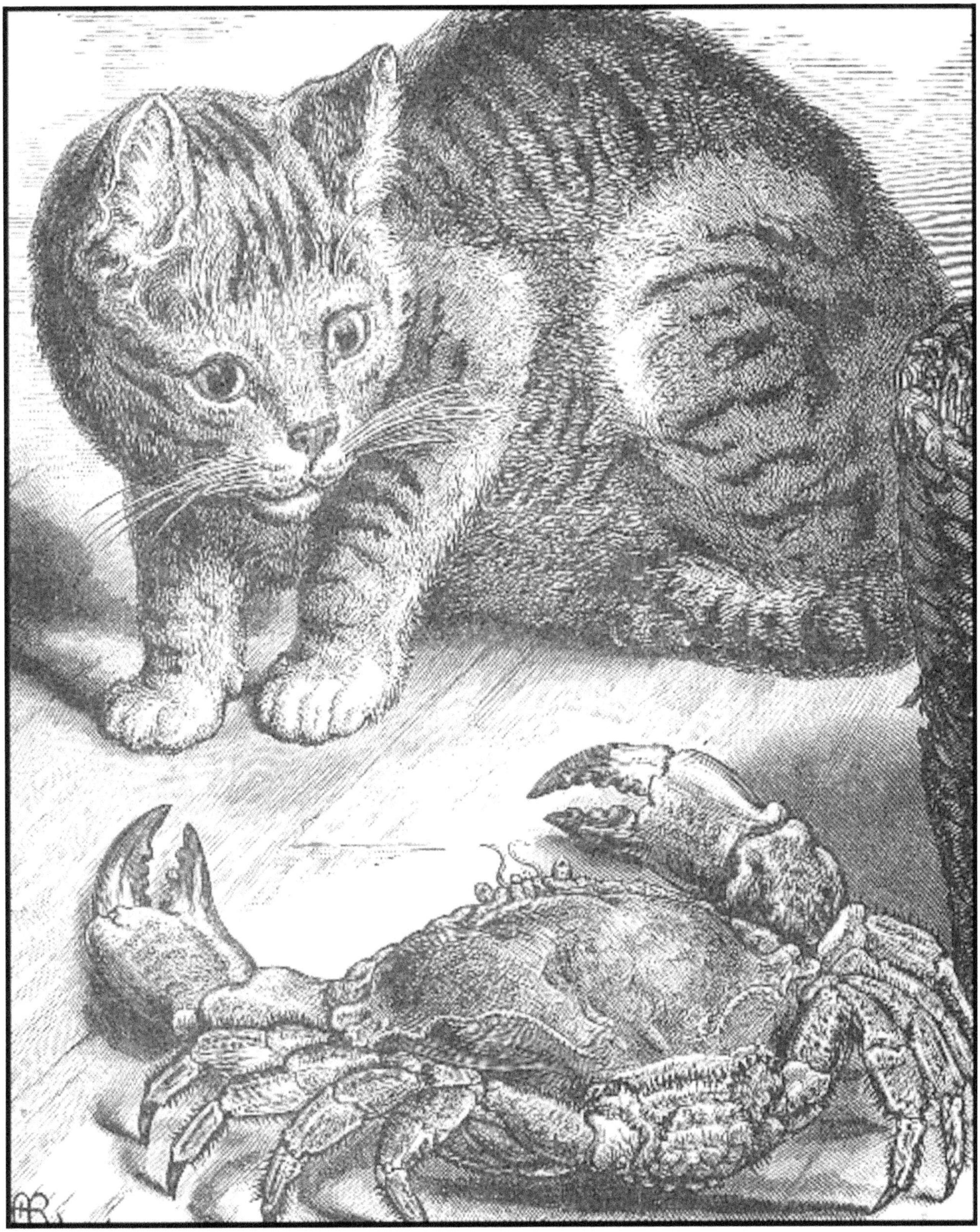

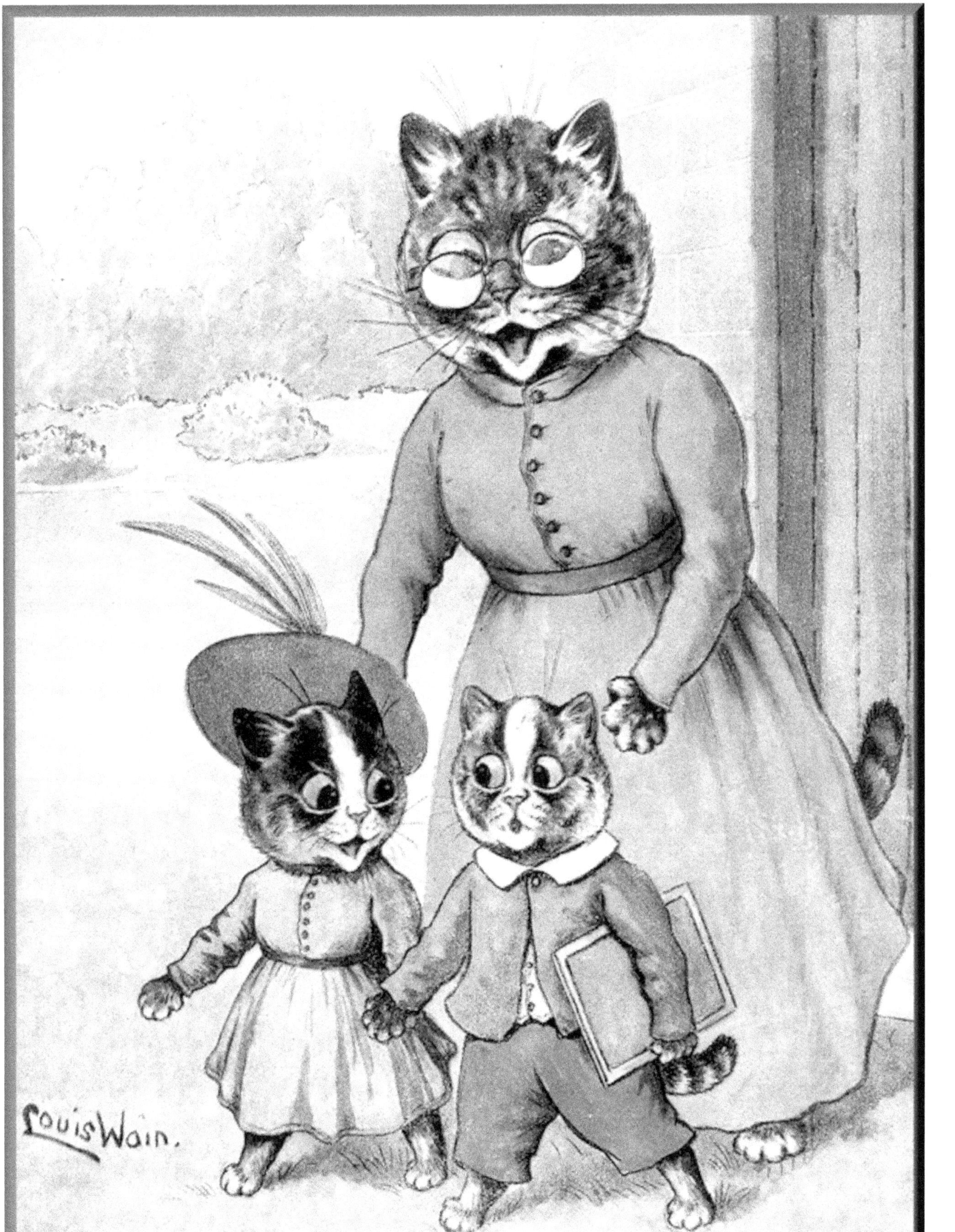
Louis Wain.

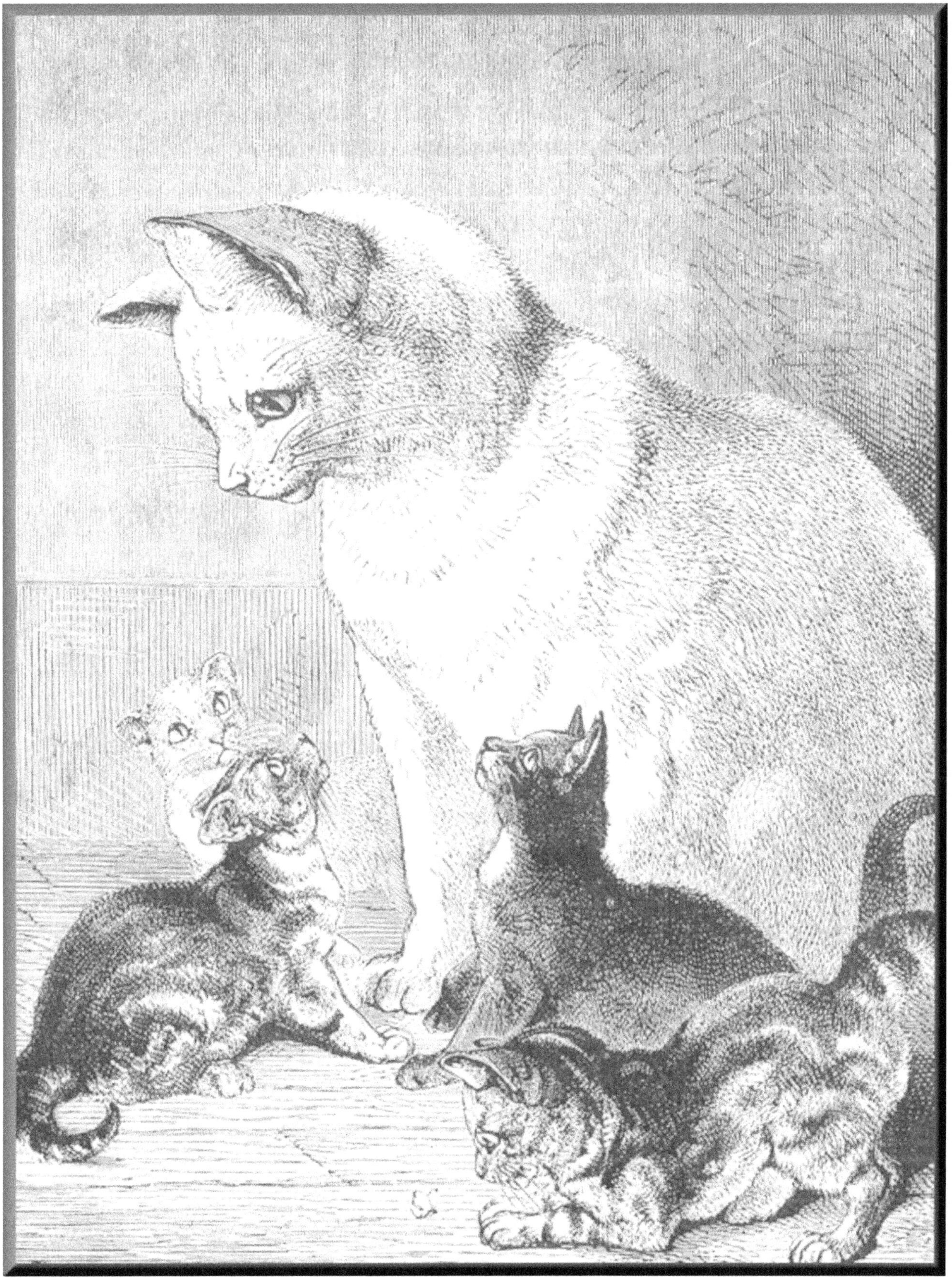

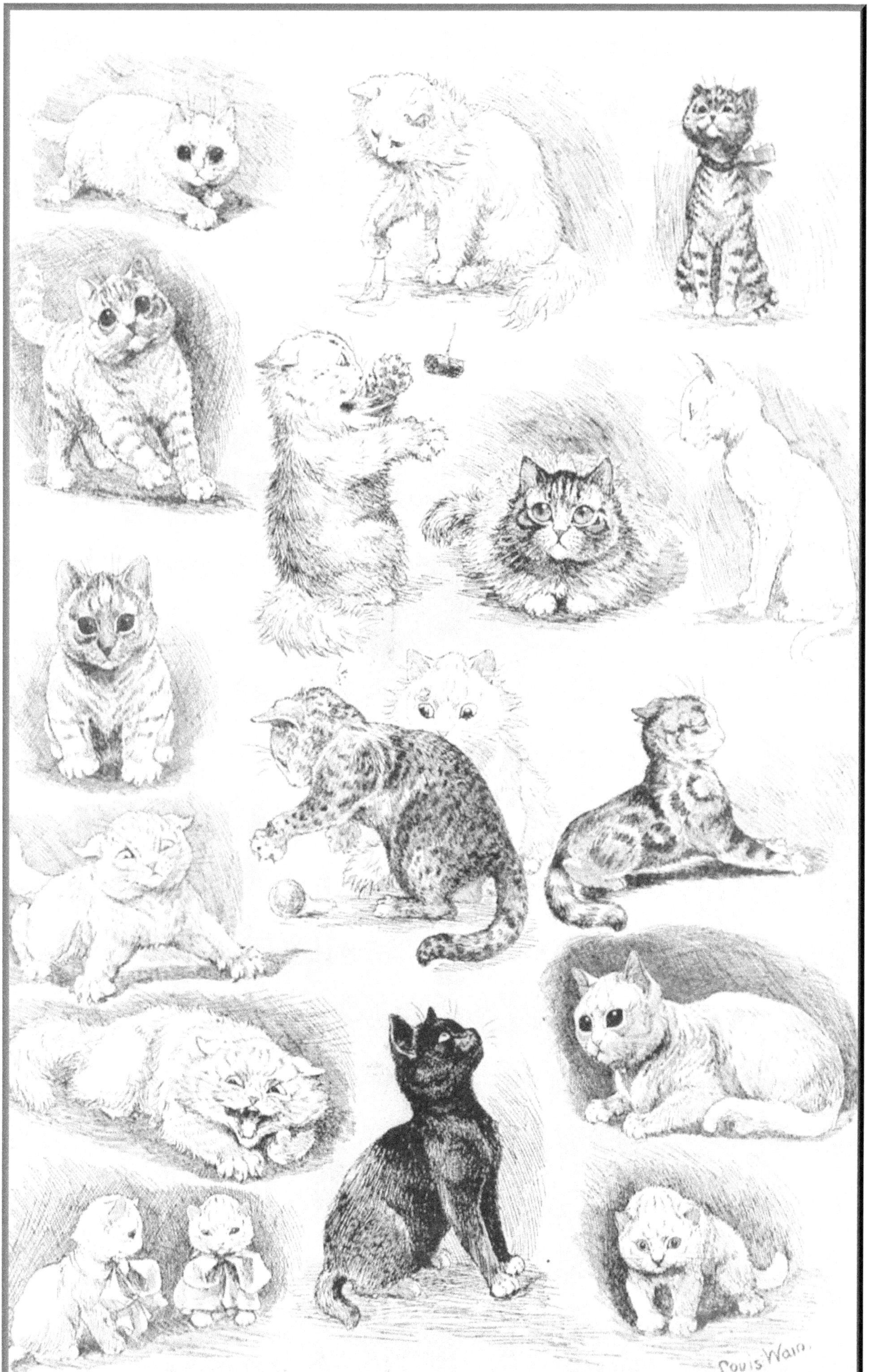
Louis Wain.

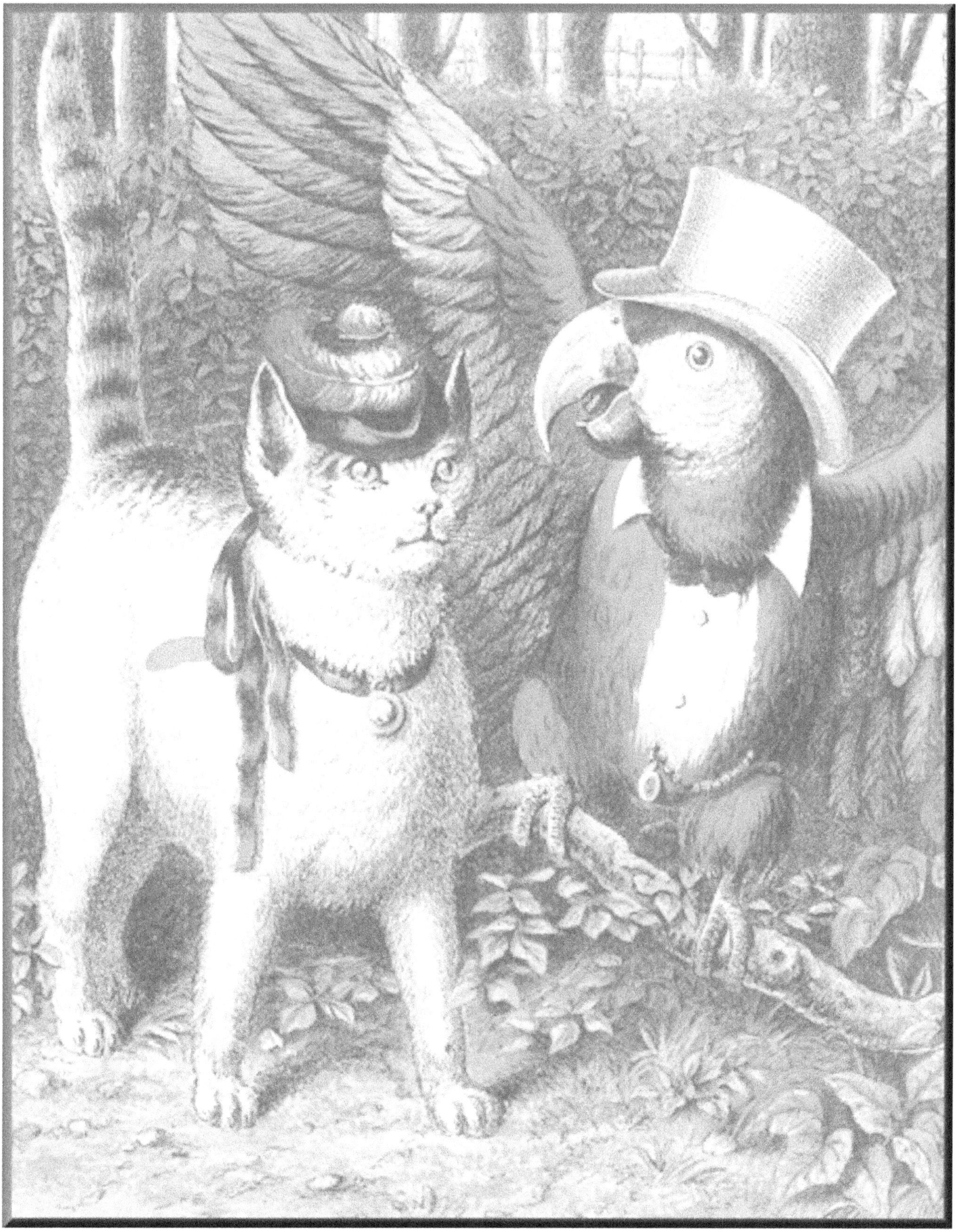

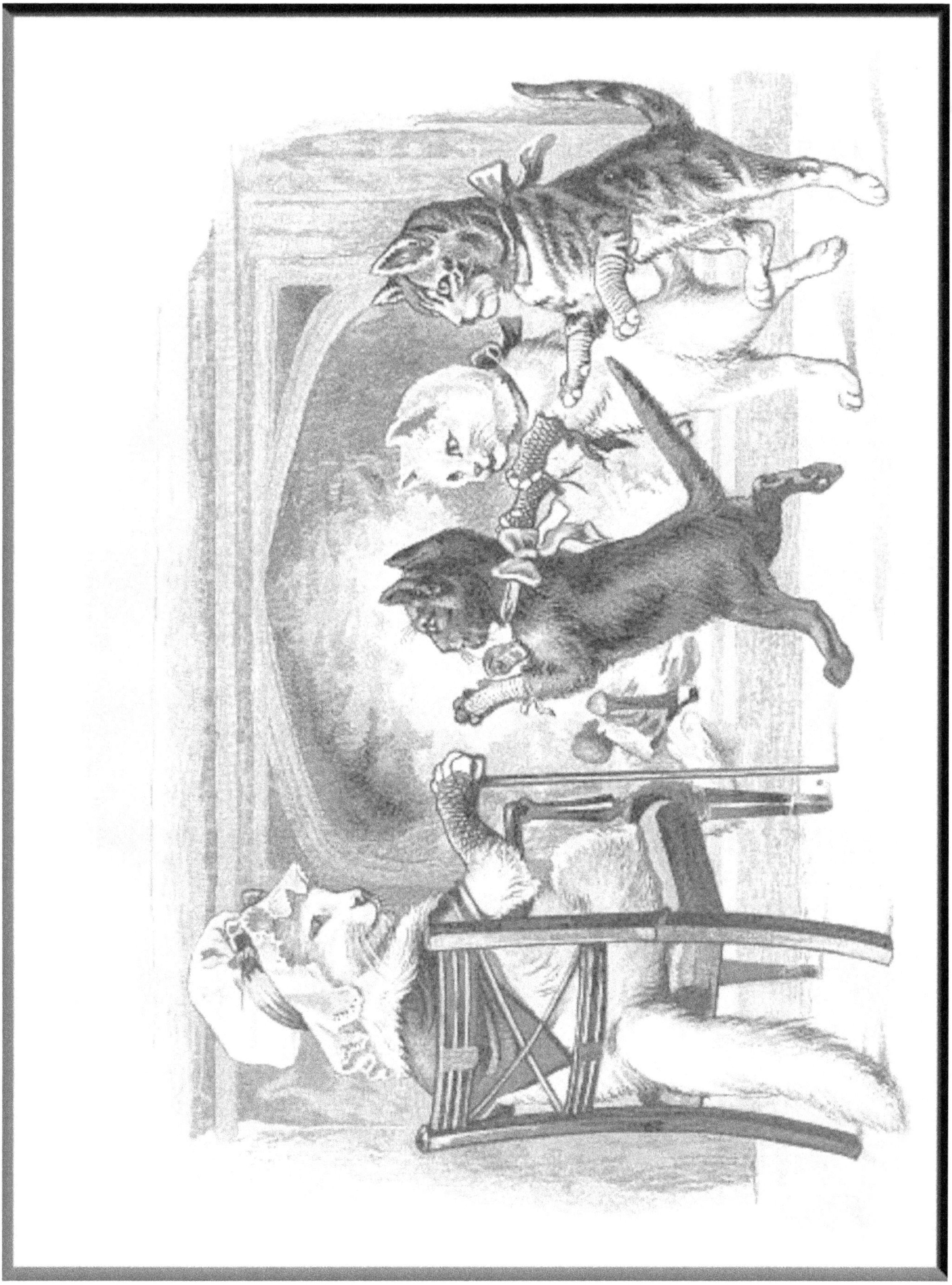

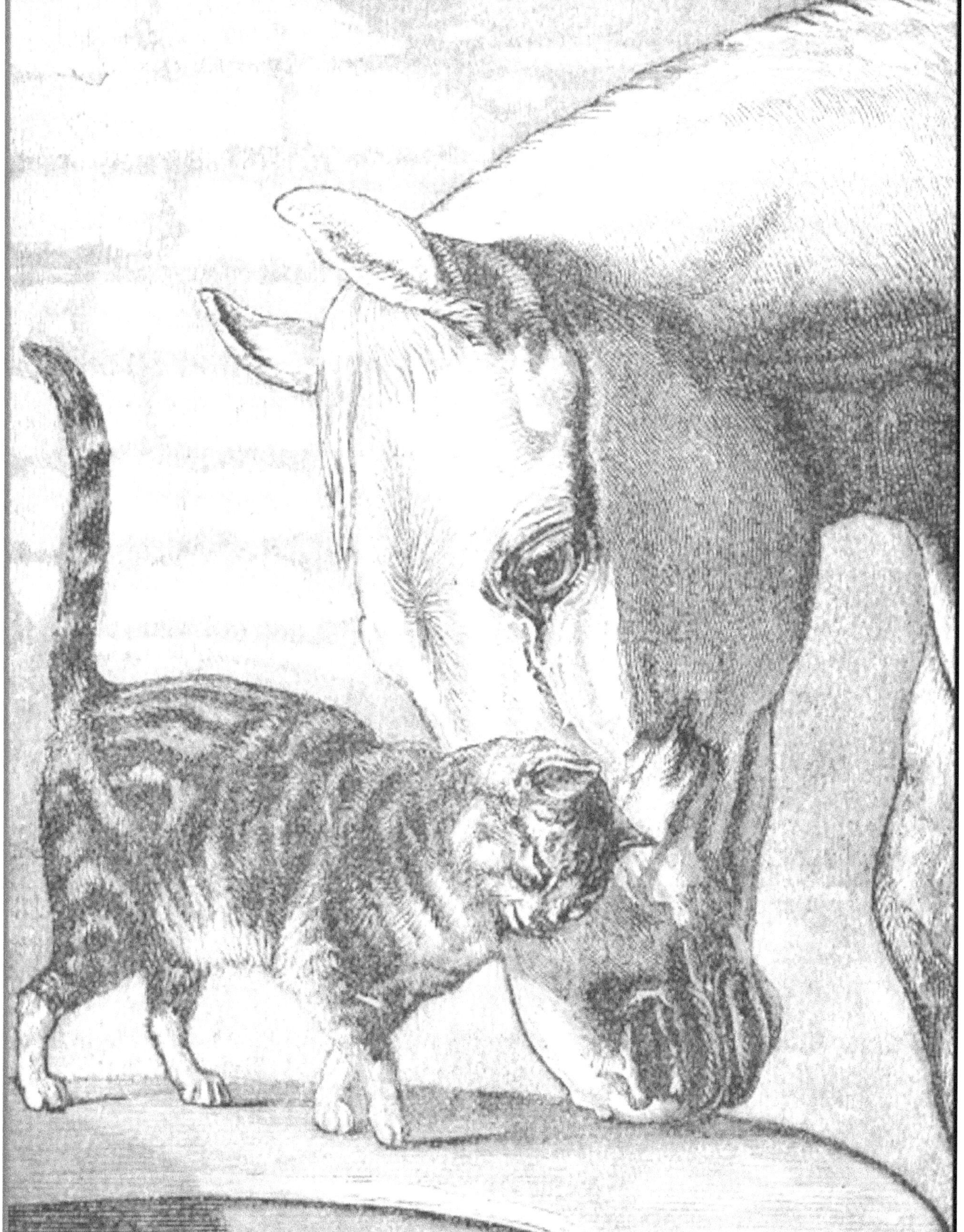

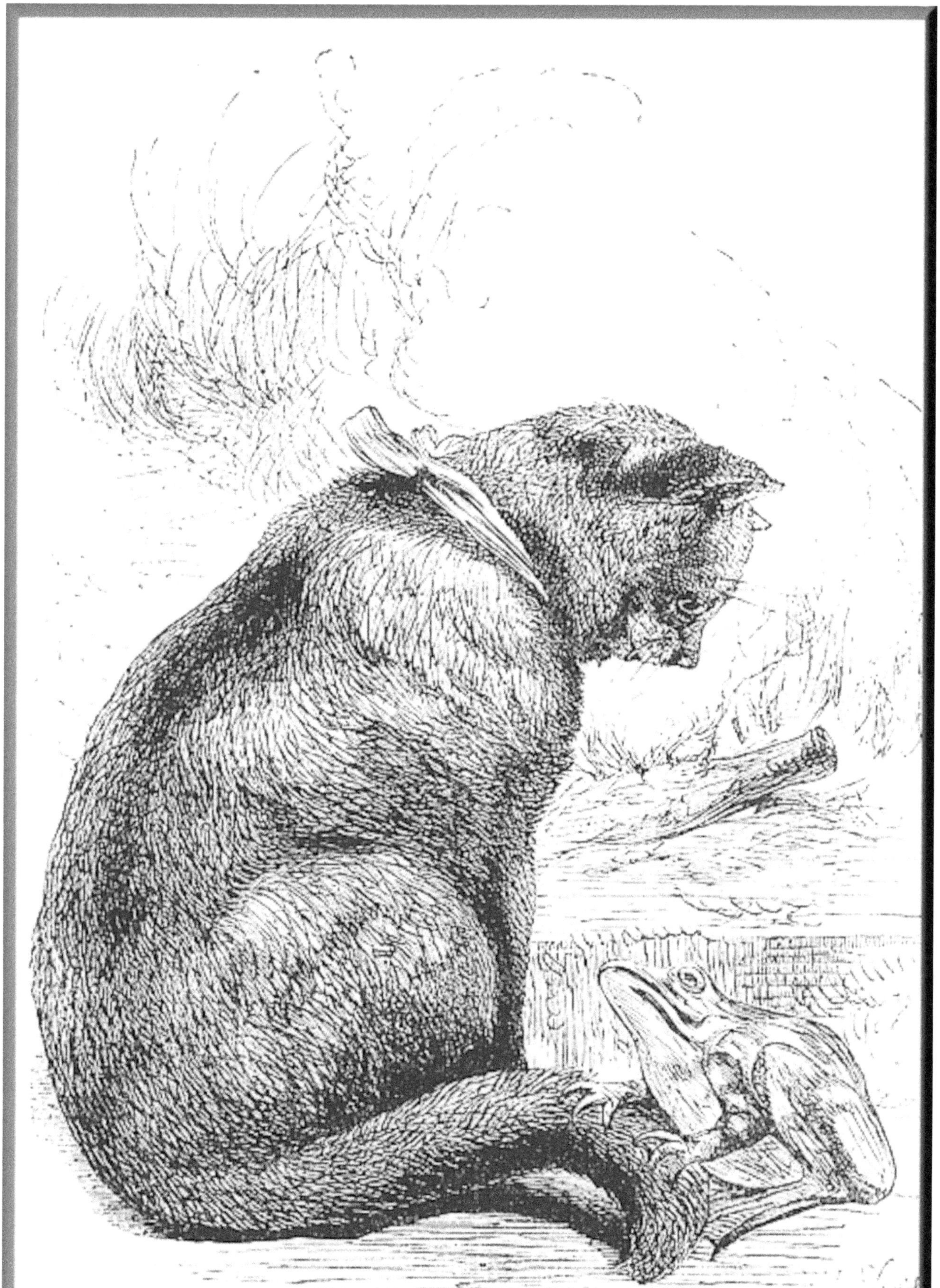

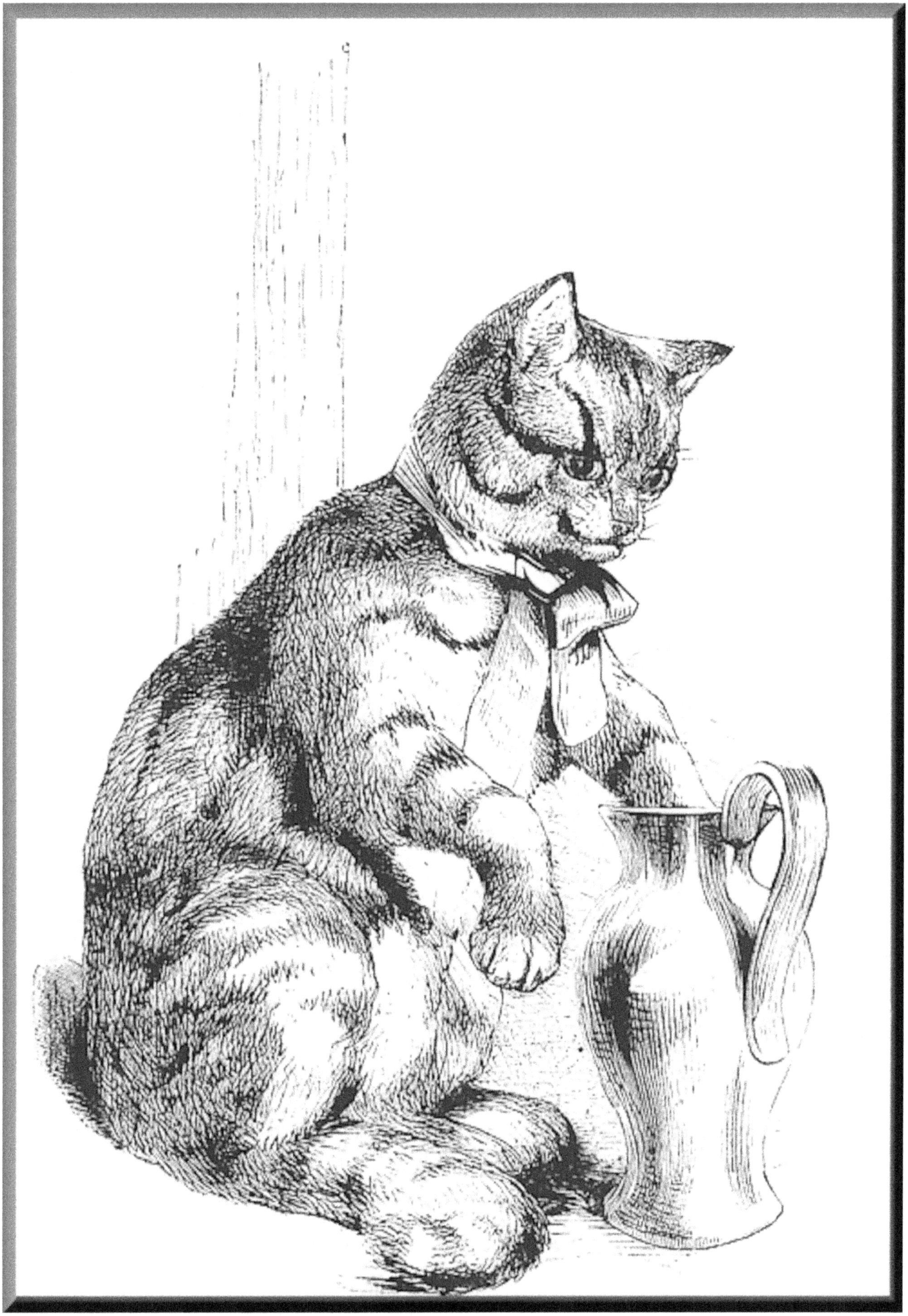

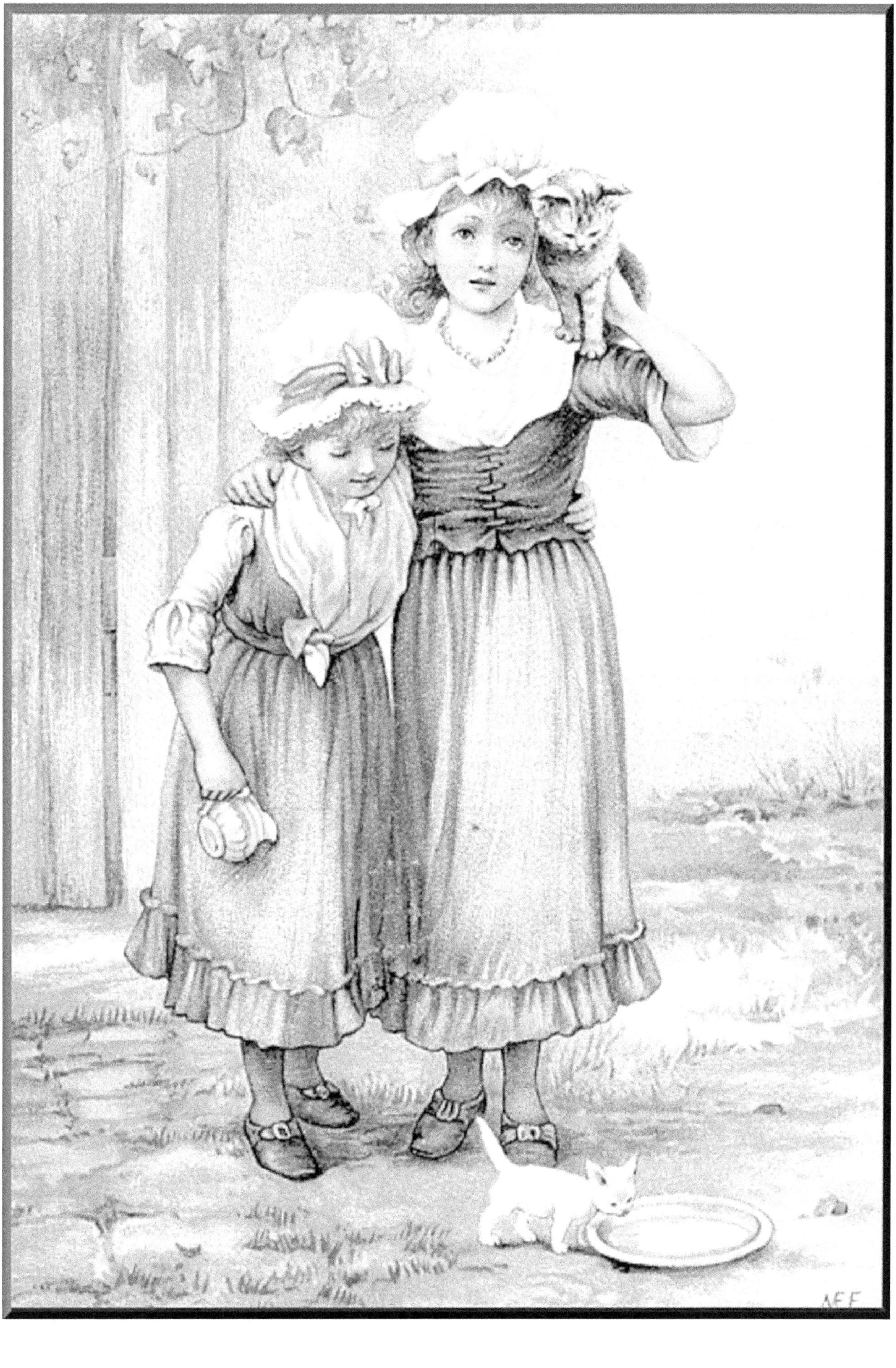

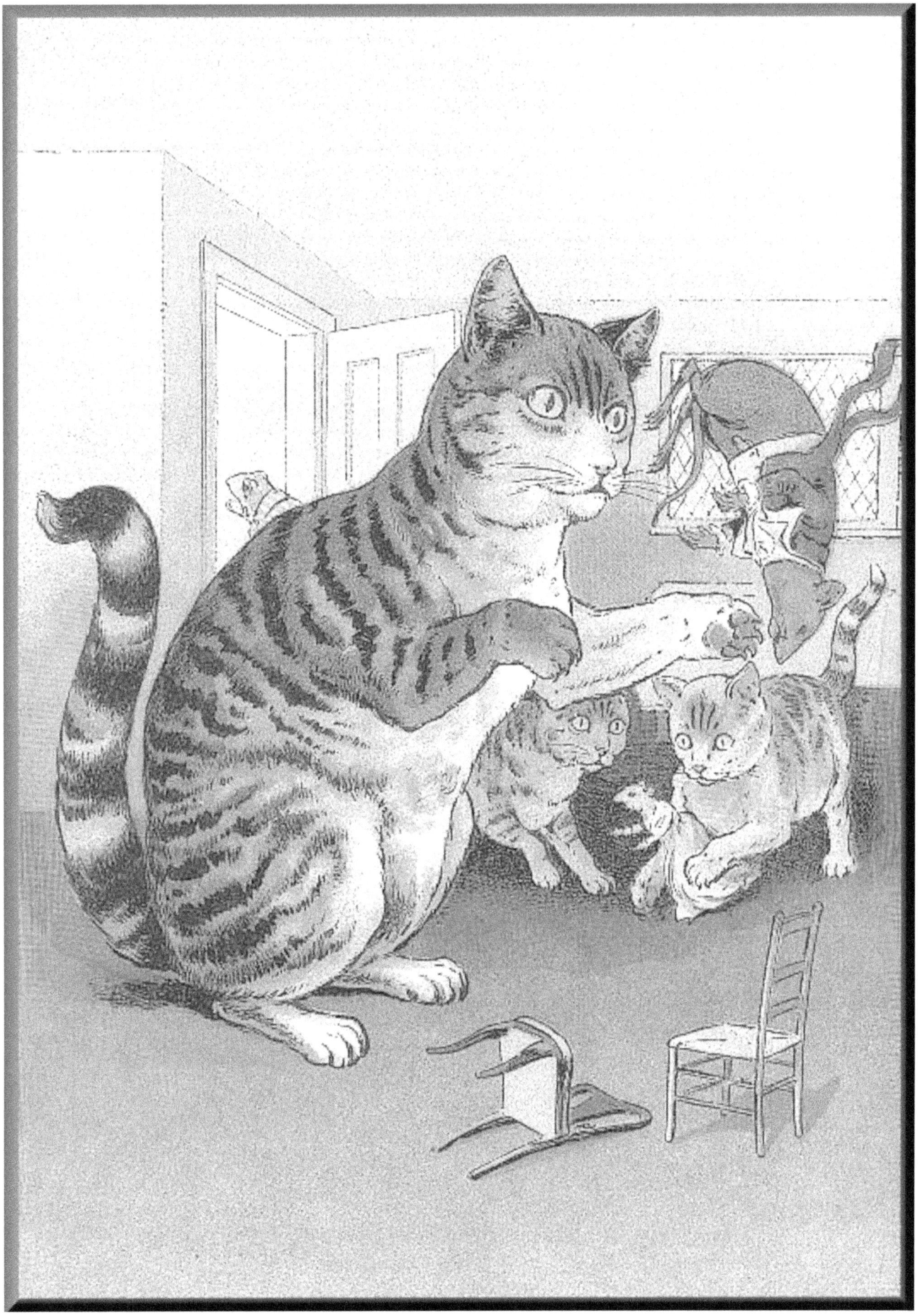

www.ingramcontent.com/pod-product-compliance
Lightning Source LLC
Chambersburg PA
CBHW080537190526
45169CB00007B/2534
9781534688858